Colorado Rockies 2021

A Baseball Companion

Edited by Steven Goldman and Bret Sayre

Baseball Prospectus

Craig Brown, Associate Editor
Robert Au, Harry Pavlidis and Amy Pircher, Statistics Editors

Copyright © 2021 by DIY Baseball, LLC.
All rights reserved

This book or any part thereof may not be reproduced or transmitted in any form or by any means, electronic or mechanical, including photocopying, recording, or by any information storage and retrieval system, without permission in writing from the publisher.

Limit of Liability/Disclaimer of Warranty: While the publisher and the author have used their best efforts in preparing this book, they make no representations or warranties with respect to the accuracy or completeness of the contents of this book and specifically disclaim any implied warranties of merchantability or fitness for a particular purpose. No warranty may be created or extended by sales representatives or written sales materials. The advice and strategies contained herein may not be suitable for your situation. You should consult with a professional where appropriate. Neither the publisher nor the author shall be liable for any loss of profit or any other commercial damages, including but not limited to special, incidental, consequential, or other damages.

Library of Congress Cataloging-in-Publication Data:
paperback
ISBN-13: 978-1-950716-41-8

Project Credits
Cover Design: Ginny Searle
Interior Design and Production: Amy Pircher, Robert Au
Layout: Amy Pircher, Robert Au

Baseball icon courtesy of Uberux, from https://www.shareicon.net/author/uberux

Ballpark diagram courtesy of Lou Spirito/THIRTY81 Project, https://thirty81project.com/

Manufactured in the United States of America
10 9 8 7 6 5 4 3 2 1

Table of Contents

Statistical Introduction v

Part 1: Team Analysis

Performance Graphs 3
2020 Team Performance 4
2021 Team Projections 5
Team Personnel 6
Coors Field Stats 7
Rockies Team Analysis 9

Part 2: Player Analysis

Rockies Player Analysis 16
Rockies Prospects 85

Part 3: Featured Articles

Rockies All-Time Top 10 Players 97
    by Steven Goldman

A Taxonomy of 2020 Abnormalities 105
    by Rob Mains

Tranches of WAR 111
    by Russell A. Carleton

Secondhand Sport 117
    by Patrick Dubuque

Steve Dalkowski Dreaming 121
    by Steven Goldman

A Reward For A Functioning Society 125
    by Cory Frontin and Craig Goldstein

Index of Names 129

Statistical Introduction

Sports are, fundamentally, a blend of athletic endeavor and storytelling. Baseball, like any other sport, tells its stories in so many ways: in the arc of a game from the stands or a season from the box scores, in photos, or even in numbers. At Baseball Prospectus, we understand that statistics don't replace observation or any of baseball's stories, but complement everything else that makes the game so much fun.

What stats help us with is with patterns and precision, variance and value. This book can help you learn things you may not see from watching a game or hundred, whether it's the path of a career over time or the breadth of the entire MLB. We'd also never ask you to choose between our numbers and the experience of viewing a game from the cheap seats or the comfort of your home; our publication combines running the numbers with observations and wisdom from some of the brightest minds we can find. But if you *do* want to learn more about the numbers beyond what's on the backs of player jerseys, let us help explain.

Offense

We've revised our methodology for determining batting value. Long-time readers of the book will notice that we've retired True Average in favor of a new metric: Deserved Runs Created Plus (DRC+). Developed by Jonathan Judge and our stats team, this statistic measures everything a player does at the plate–reaching base, hitting for power, making outs, and moving runners over–and puts it on a scale where 100 equals league-average performance. A DRC+ of 150 is terrific, a DRC+ of 100 is average and a DRC+ of 75 means you better be an excellent defender.

DRC+ also does a better job than any of our previous metrics in taking contextual factors into account. The model adjusts for how the park affects performance, but also for things like the talent of the opposing pitcher, value of different types of batted-ball events, league, temperature and other factors. It's able to describe a player's expected offensive contribution than any other statistic we've found over the years, and also does a better job of predicting future performance as well.

The other aspect of run-scoring is baserunning, which we quantify using Baserunning Runs. BRR not only records the value of stolen bases (or getting caught in the act), but also accounts for all the stuff that doesn't show up on the back of a baseball card: a runner's ability to go first to third on a single, or advance on a fly ball.

Defense

Where offensive value is *relatively* easy to identify and understand, defensive value is … not. Over the past dozen years, the sabermetric community has focused mostly on stats based on zone data: a real-live human person records the type of batted ball and estimated landing location, and models are created that give expected outs. From there, you can compare fielders' actual outs to those expected ones. Simple, right?

Unfortunately, zone data has two major issues. First, zone data is recorded by commercial data providers who keep the raw data private unless you pay for it. (All the statistics we build in this book and on our website use public data as inputs.) That hurts our ability to test assumptions or duplicate results. Second, over the years it has become apparent that there's quite a bit of "noise" in zone-based fielding analysis. Sometimes the conclusions drawn from zone data don't hold up to scrutiny, and sometimes the different data provided by different providers don't look anything alike, giving wildly different results. Sometimes the hard-working professional stringers or scorers might unknowingly inflict unconscious bias into the mix: for example good fielders will often be credited with more expected outs despite the data, and ballparks with high press boxes tend to score more line drives than ones with a lower press box.

Enter our Fielding Runs Above Average (FRAA). For most positions, FRAA is built from play-by-play data, which allows us to avoid the subjectivity found in many other fielding metrics. The idea is this: count how many fielding plays are made by a given player and compare that to expected plays for an average fielder at their position (based on pitcher ground ball tendencies and batter handedness). Then we adjust for park and base-out situations.

When it comes to catchers, our methodology is a little different thanks to the laundry list of responsibilities they're tasked with beyond just, well, catching and throwing the ball. By now you've probably heard about "framing" or the art of making umpires more likely to call balls outside the strike zone for strikes. To put this into one tidy number, we incorporate pitch tracking data (for the years it exists) and adjust for important factors like pitcher, umpire, batter and home-field advantage using a mixed-model approach. This grants us a number for how many strikes the catcher is personally adding to (or subtracting from) his pitchers' performance … which we then convert to runs added or lost using linear weights.

Framing is one of the biggest parts of determining catcher value, but we also take into account blocking balls from going past, whether a scorer deems it a passed ball or a wild pitch. We use a similar approach—one that really benefits from the pitch tracking data that tells us what ends up in the dirt and what doesn't. We also include a catcher's ability to prevent stolen bases and how well they field balls in play, and *finally* we come up with our FRAA for catchers.

Pitching

Both pitching and fielding make up the half of baseball that isn't run scoring: run prevention. Separating pitching from fielding is a tough task, and most recent pitching analysis has branched off from Voros McCracken's famous (and controversial) statement, "There is little if any difference among major-league pitchers in their ability to prevent hits on balls hit in the field of play." The research of the analytic community has validated this to some extent, and there are a host of "defense-independent" pitching measures that have been developed to try and extract the effect of the defense behind a hurler from the pitcher's work.

Our solution to this quandary is Deserved Run Average (DRA), our core pitching metric. DRA seeks to evaluate a pitcher's performance, much like earned run average (ERA), the tried-and-true pitching stat you've seen on every baseball broadcast or box score from the past century, but it's very different. To start, DRA takes an event-by-event look at what the pitchers does, and adjusts the value of that event based on different environmental factors like park, batter, catcher, umpire, base-out situation, run differential, inning, defense, home field advantage, pitcher role and temperature. That mixed model gives us a pitcher's expected contribution, similar to what we do for our DRC+ model for hitters and FRAA model for catchers. (Oh, and we also consider the pitcher's effect on basestealing and on balls getting past the catcher.)

DRA is set to the scale of runs allowed per nine innings (RA9) instead of ERA, which makes DRA's scale slightly higher than ERA's. Because of this, for ease of use, we're supplying DRA-, which is much easier for the reader to parse. As with DRC+, DRA- is an "index" stat, meaning instead of using some arbitrary and shifting number to denote what's "good," average is always 100. The reason that it uses a minus rather than a plus is because like ERA, a lower number is better. Therefore a 75 DRA- describes a performance 25 percent better than average, whereas a 150 DRA- means that either a pitcher is getting extremely lucky with their results, or getting ready to try a new pitch.

Since the last time you picked up an edition of this book, we've also made a few minor changes to DRA to make it better. Recent research into "tunneling"—the act of throwing consecutive pitches that appear similar from a batter's point of view until after the swing decision point–data has given us a new contextual factor to account for in DRA: plate distance. This refers to the distance between successive pitches as they approach the plate, and while it has a smaller effect than factors like velocity or whiff rate, it still can help explain pitcher strikeout rate in our model.

Recently Added Descriptive Statistics

Returning to our 2021 edition of the book are a few figures which recently appeared. These numbers may be a little bit more familiar to those of you who have spent some time investigating baseball statistics.

Fastball Percentage

Our fastball percentage (FA%) statistic measures how frequently a pitcher throws a pitch classified as a "fastball," measured as a percentage of overall pitches thrown. We qualify three types of fastballs:

1. The traditional four-seam fastball;
2. The two-seam fastball or sinker;
3. "Hard cutters," which are pitches that have the movement profile of a cut fastball and are used as the pitcher's primary offering or in place of a more traditional fastball.

For example, a pitcher with a FA% of 67 throws any combination of these three pitches about two-thirds of the time.

Whiff Rate

Everybody loves a swing and a miss, and whiff rate (Whiff%) measures how frequently pitchers induce a swinging strike. To calculate Whiff%, we add up all the pitches thrown that ended with a swinging strike, then divide that number by a pitcher's total pitches thrown. Most often, high whiff rates correlate with high strikeout rates (and overall effective pitcher performance).

Called Strike Probability

Called Strike Probability (CSP) is a number that represents the likelihood that all of a pitcher's pitches will be called a strike while controlling for location, pitcher and batter handedness, umpire and count. Here's how it works: on each pitch, our model determines how many times (out of 100) that a similar pitch was called for a strike given those factors mentioned above, and when normalized for each batter's strike zone. Then we average the CSP for all pitches thrown by a pitcher in a season, and that gives us the yearly CSP percentage you see in the stats boxes.

As you might imagine, pitchers with a higher CSP are more likely to work in the zone, where pitchers with a lower CSP are likely locating their pitches outside the normal strike zone, for better or for worse.

Projections

Many of you aren't turning to this book just for a look at what a player has done, but for a look at what a player is going to do: the PECOTA projections. PECOTA, initially developed by Nate Silver (who has moved on to greater fame as a political analyst), consists of three parts:

1. Major-league equivalencies, which use minor-league statistics to project how a player will perform in the major leagues;
2. Baseline forecasts, which use weighted averages and regression to the mean to estimate a player's current true talent level; and
3. Aging curves, which uses the career paths of comparable players to estimate how a player's statistics are likely to change over time.

With all those important things covered, let's take a look at what's in the book this year.

Team Prospectus

Most of this book is composed of team chapters, with one for each of the 30 major-league franchises. On the first page of each chapter, you'll see a box that contains some of the key statistics for each team as well as a very inviting stadium diagram.

We start with the team name, their unadjusted 2020 win-loss record, and their divisional ranking. Beneath that are a host of other team statistics. **Pythag** presents an adjusted 2020 winning percentage, calculated by taking runs scored per game (**RS/G**) and runs allowed per game (**RA/G**) for the team, and running them through a version of Bill James' Pythagorean formula that was refined and improved by David Smyth and Brandon Heipp. (The formula is called "Pythagenpat," which is equally fun to type and to say.)

Next up is **DRC+**, described earlier, to indicate the overall hitting ability of the team either above or below league-average. Run prevention on the pitching side is covered by **DRA** (also mentioned earlier) and another metric: Fielding Independent Pitching (**FIP**), which calculates another ERA-like statistic based on strikeouts, walks, and home runs recorded. Defensive Efficiency Rating (**DER**) tells us the percentage of balls in play turned into outs for the team, and is a quick fielding shorthand that rounds out run prevention.

After that, we have several measures related to roster composition, as opposed to on-field performance. **B-Age** and **P-Age** tell us the average age of a team's batters and pitchers, respectively. **Payroll** is the combined team payroll for all on-field players, and Doug Pappas' Marginal Dollars per Marginal Win (**M$/MW**) tells us how much money a team spent to earn production above replacement level.

Next to each of these stats, we've listed each team's MLB rank in that category from first to 30th. In this, first always indicates a positive outcome and 30th a negative outcome, except in the case of salary—first is highest.

After the franchise statistics, we share a few items about the team's home ballpark. There's the aforementioned diagram of the park's dimensions (including distances to the outfield wall), a graphic showing the height of the wall from the left-field pole to the right-field pole, and a table showing three-year park factors for the stadium. The park factors are displayed as indexes where 100 is average, 110 means that the park inflates the statistic in question by 10 percent, and 90 means that the park deflates the statistic in question by 10 percent.

On the second page of each team chapter, you'll find three graphs. The first is **Payroll History** and helps you see how the team's payroll has compared to the MLB and divisional average payrolls over time. Payroll figures are current as of January 1, 2021; with so many free agents still unsigned as of this writing, the final 2021 figure will likely be significantly different for many teams. (In the meantime, you can always find the most current data at Baseball Prospectus' Cot's Baseball Contracts page.)

The second graph is **Future Commitments** and helps you see the team's future outlays, if any.

The third graph is **Farm System Ranking** and displays how the Baseball Prospectus prospect team has ranked the organization's farm system since 2007.

After the graphs, we have a **Personnel** section that lists many of the important decision-makers and upper-level field and operations staff members for the franchise, as well as any former Baseball Prospectus staff members who are currently part of the organization. (In very rare circumstances, someone might be on both lists!)

Position Players

After all that information and a thoughtful bylined essay covering each team, we present our player comments. These are also bylined, but due to frequent franchise shifts during the offseason, our bylines are more a rough guide than a perfect accounting of who wrote what.

Each player is listed with the major-league team that employed him as of early January 2021. If a player changed teams after that point via free agency, trade, or any other method, you'll be able to find them in the chapter for their previous squad.

As an example, take a look at the player comment for Padres shortstop Fernando Tatis Jr.: the stat block that accompanies his written comment is at the top of this page. First we cover biographical information (age is as of June 30, 2021) before moving onto the stats themselves. Our statistic columns include standard identifying information like **YEAR**, **TEAM**, **LVL** (level of affiliated play) and **AGE** before getting into the numbers. Next, we provide raw, untranslated

Fernando Tatis Jr. SS

Born: 01/02/99 Age: 22 Bats: R Throws: R
Height: 6'3" Weight: 217 Origin: International Free Agent, 2015

YEAR	TEAM	LVL	AGE	PA	R	2B	3B	HR	RBI	BB	K	SB	CS	AVG/OBP/SLG
2018	SA	AA	19	394	77	22	4	16	43	33	109	16	5	.286/.355/.507
2019	SD	MLB	20	372	61	13	6	22	53	30	110	16	6	.317/.379/.590
2020	SD	MLB	21	257	50	11	2	17	45	27	61	11	3	.277/.366/.571
2021 FS	SD	MLB	22	600	95	24	4	31	81	50	165	17	8	.263/.331/.499
2021 DC	SD	MLB	22	628	100	25	4	32	85	53	173	19	8	.263/.331/.499

Comparables: Darryl Strawberry, Bo Bichette, Ronald Acuña Jr.

YEAR	TEAM	LVL	AGE	PA	DRC+	BABIP	BRR	FRAA	WARP
2018	SA	AA	19	394	136	.370	3.0	SS(83): -1.9	2.4
2019	SD	MLB	20	372	118	.410	7.1	SS(83): 0.9	3.4
2020	SD	MLB	21	257	126	.306	0.7	SS(57): -5.5	0.9
2021 FS	SD	MLB	22	600	126	.318	1.7	SS -1	3.9
2021 DC	SD	MLB	22	628	126	.318	1.8	SS -1	4.0

numbers like you might find on the back of your dad's baseball cards: **PA** (plate appearances), **R** (runs), **2B** (doubles), **3B** (triples), **HR** (home runs), **RBI** (runs batted in), **BB** (walks), **K** (strikeouts), **SB** (stolen bases) and **CS** (caught stealing).

Following the basic stats is **Whiff%** (whiff rate), which denotes how often, when a batter swings, he fails to make contact with the ball. Another way to think of this number is an inverse of a hitter's contact rate.

Next, we have unadjusted "slash" statistics: **AVG** (batting average), **OBP** (on-base percentage) and **SLG** (slugging percentage). Following the slash line is **DRC+** (Deserved Runs Created Plus), which we described earlier as total offensive expected contribution compared to the league average.

BABIP (batting average on balls in play) tells us how often a ball in play fell for a hit, and can help us identify whether a batter may have been lucky or not ... but note that high BABIPs also tend to follow the great hitters of our time, as well as speedy singles hitters who put the ball on the ground.

The next item is **BRR** (Baserunning Runs), which covers all of a player's baserunning accomplishments including (but not limited to) swiped bags and failed attempts. Next is **FRAA** (Fielding Runs Above Average), which also includes the number of games previously played at each position noted in parentheses. Multi-position players have only their two most frequent positions listed here, but their total FRAA number reflects all positions played.

Our last column here is **WARP** (Wins Above Replacement Player). WARP estimates the total value of a player, which means for hitters it takes into account hitting runs above average (calculated using the DRC+ model), BRR and FRAA. Then, it makes an adjustment for positions played and gives the player a credit for plate appearances based upon the difference between "replacement level"—which is derived from the quality of players added to a team's roster after the start of the season–and the league average.

The final line just below the stats box is **PECOTA** data, which is discussed further in a following section.

Catchers

Catchers are a special breed, and thus they have earned their own separate box which displays some of the defensive metrics that we've built just for them. As an example, let's check out Yasmani Grandal.

YEAR	TEAM	P. COUNT	FRM RUNS	BLK RUNS	THRW RUNS	TOT RUNS
2018	LAD	16816	15.7	0.8	0.1	16.5
2019	MIL	18740	19.4	1.8	-0.1	21.1
2020	CHW	4830	3.7	0.3	-0.2	3.8
2021	CHW	14430	16.7	-0.6	1.0	17.1
2021	CHW	14430	16.7	0.4	1.0	18.0

The **YEAR** and **TEAM** columns match what you'd find in the other stat box. **P. COUNT** indicates the number of pitches thrown while the catcher was behind the plate, including swinging strikes, fouls and balls in play. **FRM RUNS** is the total run value the catcher provided (or cost) his team by influencing the umpire to call strikes where other catchers did not. **BLK RUNS** expresses the total run value above or below average for the catcher's ability to prevent wild pitches and passed balls. **THRW RUNS** is calculated using a similar model as the previous two statistics, and it measures a catcher's ability to throw out basestealers but also to dissuade them from testing his arm in the first place. It takes into account factors like the pitcher (including his delivery and pickoff move) and baserunner (who could be as fast as Billy Hamilton or as slow as Yonder Alonso). **TOT RUNS** is the sum of all of the previous three statistics.

Pitchers

Let's give our pitchers a turn, using 2020 AL Cy Young winner Shane Bieber as our example. Take a look at his stat block: the first line and the **YEAR**, **TEAM**, **LVL** and **AGE** columns are the same as in the position player example earlier.

Here too, we have a series of columns that display raw, unadjusted statistics compiled by the pitcher over the course of a season: **W** (wins), **L** (losses), **SV** (saves), **G** (games pitched), **GS** (games started), **IP** (innings pitched), **H** (hits allowed) and **HR** (home runs allowed). Next we have two statistics that are rates: **BB/9** (walks per nine innings) and **K/9** (strikeouts per nine innings), before returning to the unadjusted **K** (strikeouts).

Next up is **GB%** (ground ball percentage), which is the percentage of all batted balls that were hit on the ground, including both outs and hits. Remember, this is based on observational data and subject to human error, so please approach this with a healthy dose of skepticism.

BABIP (batting average on balls in play) is calculated using the same methodology as it is for position players, but it often tells us more about a pitcher than it does a hitter. With pitchers, a high BABIP is often due to poor defense or bad luck, and can often be an indicator of potential rebound, and a low BABIP may be cause to expect performance regression. (A typical league-average BABIP is close to .290-.300.)

The metrics **WHIP** (walks plus hits per inning pitched) and **ERA** (earned run average) are old standbys: WHIP measures walks and hits allowed on a per-inning basis, while ERA measures earned runs on a nine-inning basis. Neither of these stats are translated or adjusted.

DRA- (Deserved Run Average) was described at length earlier, and measures how the pitcher "deserved" to perform compared to other pitchers. Please note that since we lack all the data points that would make for a "real" DRA for minor-league events, the DRA- displayed for minor league partial-seasons is based off of different data. (That data is a modified version of our cFIP metric, which you can find more information about on our website.)

Shane Bieber   RHP

Born: 05/31/95   Age: 26   Bats: R   Throws: R
Height: 6'3"   Weight: 200   Origin: Round 4, 2016 Draft (#122 overall)

YEAR	TEAM	LVL	AGE	W	L	SV	G	GS	IP	H	HR	BB/9	K/9	K	GB%	BABIP
2018	AKR	AA	23	3	0	0	5	5	31	26	1	0.3	8.7	30	47.3%	.278
2018	COL	AAA	23	3	1	0	8	8	48^2	30	3	1.1	8.7	47	52.0%	.227
2018	CLE	MLB	23	11	5	0	20	19	114^2	130	13	1.8	9.3	118	46.2%	.356
2019	CLE	MLB	24	15	8	0	34	33	214^1	186	31	1.7	10.9	259	44.4%	.298
2020	CLE	MLB	25	8	1	0	12	12	77^1	46	7	2.4	14.2	122	48.4%	.267
2021 FS	CLE	MLB	26	10	6	0	26	26	150	121	18	2.1	11.7	195	45.5%	.297
2021 DC	CLE	MLB	26	14	7	0	30	30	196.7	159	24	2.1	11.7	257	45.5%	.297

Comparables: Luis Severino, Danny Salazar, Joe Musgrove

YEAR	TEAM	LVL	AGE	WHIP	ERA	DRA-	WARP	MPH	FB%	WHF	CSP
2018	AKR	AA	23	0.87	1.16	61	0.9				
2018	COL	AAA	23	0.74	1.66	69	1.2				
2018	CLE	MLB	23	1.33	4.55	74	2.6	94.7	57.4%	26.2%	
2019	CLE	MLB	24	1.05	3.28	75	4.9	94.4	45.8%	30.8%	
2020	CLE	MLB	25	0.87	1.63	53	2.6	95.3	53.6%	40.7%	
2021 FS	CLE	MLB	26	1.04	2.44	64	4.4	94.7	50.0%	33.2%	44.2%
2021 DC	CLE	MLB	26	1.04	2.44	64	5.8	94.7	50.0%	33.2%	44.2%

Just like with hitters, **WARP** (Wins Above Replacement Player) is a total value metric that puts pitchers of all stripes on the same scale as position players. We use DRA as the primary input for our calculation of WARP. You might notice that relief pitchers (due to their limited innings) may have a lower WARP than you were expecting or than you might see in other WARP-like metrics. WARP does not take leverage into account, just the actions a pitcher performs and the expected value of those actions … which ends up judging high-leverage relief pitchers differently than you might imagine given their prestige and market value.

MPH gives you the pitcher's 95th percentile velocity for the noted season, in order to give you an idea of what the *peak* fastball velocity a pitcher possesses. Since this comes from our pitch-tracking data, it is not publicly available for minor-league pitchers.

Finally, we display the three new pitching metrics we described earlier. **FB%** (fastball percentage) gives you the percentage of fastballs thrown out of all pitches. **WHF** (whiff rate) tells you the percentage of swinging strikes induced out of all pitches. **CSP** (called strike probability) expresses the likelihood of all pitches thrown to result in a called strike, after controlling for factors like handedness, umpire, pitch type, count and location.

PECOTA

All players have PECOTA projections for 2021, as well as a set of other numbers that describe the performance of comparable players according to PECOTA. All projections for 2021 are for the player at the date we went to press in early January and are projected into the league and park context as indicated by the team abbreviation. (Note that players at very low levels of the minors are too unpredictable to assess using these numbers.) All PECOTA projected statistics represent a player's projected major-league performance.

How we're doing that is a little different this season. There are really two different values that go into the final stat line that you see for PECOTA: How a player performs, and how much playing time he'll be given to perform it. In the past we've estimated playing time based on each team's roster and depth charts, and we'll continue to do that. These projections are denoted as **2021 DC**.

But in many cases, a player won't be projected for major-league playing time; most of the time this is because they aren't projected to be major-league players at all, but still developing as prospects. Or perhaps a player will provide Triple-A depth, only to have an opportunity open up because of injury. For these purposes, we're also supplying a second projection, labeled **2021 FS**, or full season. This is what we would project the player to provide in 600 plate appearances or 150 innings pitched.

Below the projections are the player's three highest-scoring comparable players as determined by PECOTA. All comparables represent a snapshot of how the listed player was performing at the same age as the current player, so if a

23-year-old pitcher is compared to Bartolo Colón, he's actually being compared to a 23-year-old Colón, not the version that pitched for the Rangers in 2018, nor to Colón's career as a whole.

A few points about pitcher projections. First, we aren't yet projecting peak velocity, so that column will be blank in the PECOTA lines. Second, projecting DRA is trickier than evaluating past performance, because it is unclear how deserving each pitcher will be of his anticipated outcomes. However, we know that another DRA-related statistic–contextual FIP or cFIP–estimates future run scoring very well. So for PECOTA, the projected DRA- figures you see are based on the past cFIPs generated by the pitcher and comparable players over time, along with the other factors described above.

If you're familiar with PECOTA, then you'll have noticed that the projection system often appears bullish on players coming off a bad year and bearish on players coming off a good year. (This is because the system weights several previous seasons, not just the most recent one.) In addition, we publish the 50th percentile projections for each player–which is smack in the middle of the range of projected production—which tends to mean PECOTA stat lines don't often have extreme results like 40 home runs or 250 strikeouts in a given season. In essence, PECOTA doesn't project very many extreme seasons.

Managers

After all those wonderful team chapters, we've got statistics for each big-league manager, all of whom are organized by alphabetical order. Here you'll find a block including an extraordinary amount of information collected from each manager's entire career. For more information on the acronyms and what they mean, please visit the Glossary at www.baseballprospectus.com.

There is one important metric that we'd like to call attention to, and you'll find it next to each manager's name: **wRM+** (weighted reliever management plus). Developed by Rob Arthur and Rian Watt, wRM+ investigates how good a manager is at using their best relievers during the moments of highest leverage, using both our proprietary DRA metric as well as Leverage Index. wRM+ is scaled to a league average of 100, and a wRM+ of 105 indicates that relievers were used approximately five percent "better" than average. On the other hand, a wRM+ of 95 would tell us the team used its relievers five percent "worse" than the average team.

While wRM+ does not have an extremely strong correlation with a manager, it is statistically significant; this means that a manager is not *entirely* responsible for a team's wRM+, but does have some effect on that number.

Part 1: Team Analysis

Part 1. Teqm Analysis

Performance Graphs

Payroll History (in millions)

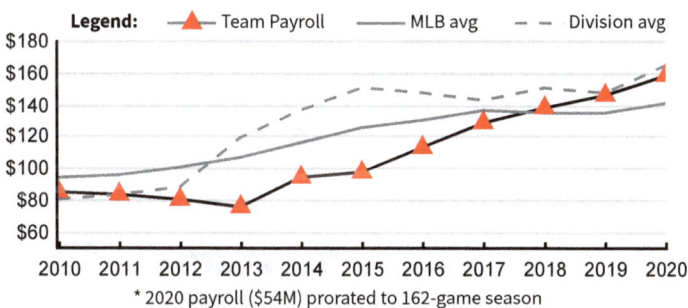

* 2020 payroll ($54M) prorated to 162-game season

Future Commitments (in millions)

Farm System Ranking

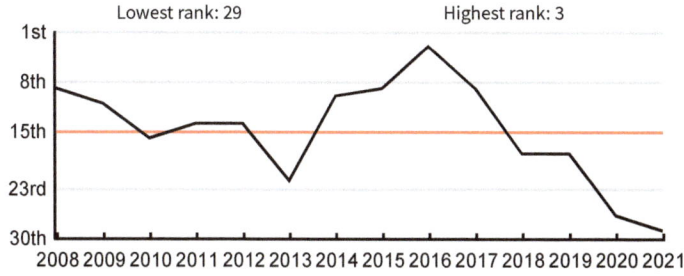

2020 Team Performance

ACTUAL STANDINGS

Team	W	L	Pct
LAD	43	17	0.717
SD	37	23	0.617
SF	29	31	0.483
COL	**26**	**34**	**0.433**
ARI	25	35	0.417

dWIN% STANDINGS

Team	W	L	Pct
LAD	37	23	0.624
SD	34	26	0.567
SF	27	33	0.465
ARI	23	37	0.386
COL	**22**	**38**	**0.375**

TOP HITTERS

Player	WARP
Nolan Arenado	1.5
Trevor Story	1.5
Charlie Blackmon	1.2

TOP PITCHERS

Player	WARP
Germán Márquez	1.7
Antonio Senzatela	0.6
Yency Almonte	0.5

VITAL STATISTICS

Statistic Name	Value	Rank
Pythagenpat	.380	28th
dWin%	.375	26th
Runs Scored per Game	4.58	15th
Runs Allowed per Game	5.88	30th
Deserved Runs Created Plus	93	26th
Deserved Run Average Minus	109	24th
Fielding Independent Pitching	5.11	28th
Defensive Efficiency Rating	.685	26th
Batter Age	29.2	23rd
Pitcher Age	27.3	4th
Payroll	$54.0M	17th
Marginal $ per Marginal Win	$4.5M	20th

2021 Team Projections

PROJECTED STANDINGS

Team	W	L	Pct	+/-
LAD	104.4	57.6	0.644	-11
With Dustin May ready and David Price returning, adding Trevor Bauer was purely lapidary. Still, they're almost alone in their willingness to put up or shut up.				
SD	95.4	66.6	0.589	-4
Not just Blake Snell, but Yu Darvish and Joe Musgrove; not just Ha-Seong Kim, but Jurickson Profar, all without trading a starting player.				
ARI	79.2	82.8	0.489	11
Mike Hazen is a good trader, but ownership continues to confine him to corner-store bartering.				
SF	74.9	87.1	0.462	-3
Most of their individual moves were small, but the Giants' winter work amounts to the first step toward pivoting from a rebuild to contending.				
COL	**58.9**	**103.1**	**0.364**	**-11**
The time was ripe for a rebuild, but the return for Nolan Arenado is not a confidence-inspiring start.				

TOP PROJECTED HITTERS

Player	WARP
Trevor Story	3.8
Charlie Blackmon	2.8
C.J. Cron	1.3

TOP PROJECTED PITCHERS

Player	WARP
Germán Márquez	2.9
Jon Gray	1.4
Kyle Freeland	1.3

FARM SYSTEM REPORT

Top Prospect	Number of Top 101 Prospects
Zac Veen, #49	1

KEY DEDUCTIONS

Player	WARP
Nolan Arenado	4.2
David Dahl	1.1

KEY ADDITIONS

Player	WARP
C.J. Cron	1.3
Austin Gomber	0.8

Team Personnel

General Manager
Jeff Bridich

Assistant General Manager - Baseball Operations
Zach Rosenthal

Assistant General Manager - Player Development
Zach Wilson

Assistant General Manager - Player Personnel
Jon Weil

Manager
Bud Black

Coors Field Stats

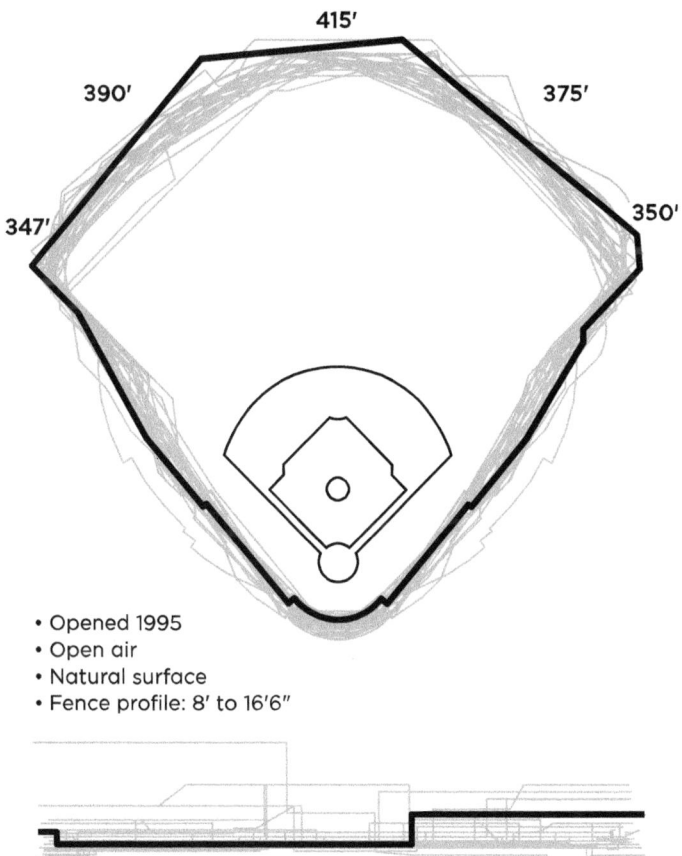

- Opened 1995
- Open air
- Natural surface
- Fence profile: 8' to 16'6"

Three-Year Park Factors

Runs	Runs/RH	Runs/LH	HR/RH	HR/LH
112	112	112	109	111

Rockies Team Analysis

There's a moment from my life as a Colorado Rockies fan that I don't like to dwell on too often, due to embarrassment. It was an hour or so before the start of Game 1 of the 2007 World Series, which the Rockies had ridden into on the back of an improbable, delirious run of games in which they were essentially unbeatable. I was 19 and preparing to watch the game with my family in a Denver bar packed with sweaty, exuberant baseball fans. My brother and I started talking about the team and decided, while quite literally high off having watched our favorite baseball team put together one of the more shocking World Series runs in history, that this was just the beginning.

We giddily reminded each other that the Rockies had Troy Tulowitzki, Matt Holliday, Garrett Atkins, Todd Helton and Brad Hawpe on the team. We had Jeff Francis and Ubaldo Jiménez and Franklin Morales, too. What we had was *a core*, a group of players that a good team could be—had been!—built around. One of us, totally giving ourselves over to the euphoria of the moment, may have even invoked the '96 Yankees as a point of comparison.

We were dumb! Extremely dumb. The Rockies would go on to get swept and humiliated by the Red Sox in that series, and the core of stud players that my brother and I had goofily marveled at was soon smashed and scattered. I bring this memory up here not because I wish to embarrass myself in front of the esteemed readers of the Baseball Prospectus Annual, but because it is an illustrative example of what it's felt like to watch the Rockies try and mostly fail to build winning baseball teams over the course of their 28-year existence.

The Rockies have always had good players. For as deranged as my brother and I may have been on that night in 2007, there is no denying the fact that Holliday, who had a 1.012 OPS in 2007 and produced 6 WAR, was a deserved NL MVP runner-up. Nor is there any denying the greatness of Tulowitzki, who had just finished his first full season as a big-leaguer by producing 6.8 WAR and establishing himself as one of the best young players in the game. You must even admit that Jeff Francis—no, sorry, nevermind, we are not talking about Jeff Francis. We are moving on!

Before that 2007 crew there was Todd Helton flirting with .400; there was Larry Walker winning the MVP on his way to the Hall of Fame; there was Andres Galarraga, Vinny Castilla and Dante Bichette being good enough to earn their nickname as The Blake Street Bombers. Pick out any Rockies roster from years past, even the ones in which the team's record was especially miserable, and more often than not you'll find yourself looking at a list that includes some legitimately good players. The Rockies have always managed to find and develop real, meaningful talent to put on the programs. They've just never been very good at completing the second step to creating a winning baseball team: actually filling out the rest of the roster with useful baseball players.

This inability to actually turn building blocks into a building has perhaps never been more obvious than it is right now. Take a look at the rosters that have been assembled by Jeff Bridich since he took over the general manager role in 2015. Over that period of time the Rockies have finished above .500 in just two seasons, both of which culminated in uninspiring playoff appearances. They have managed to do this all while having the roster anchored by a frankly excellent core of hitters.

I'm serious! This is not 19-year-old me shouting beer-soaked proclamations from a bar booth. Since 2015, Nolan Arenado, Trevor Story and Charlie Blackmon have combined to amass 69.8 WAR while wearing Rockies uniforms. Now pick basically any successful team from that same period of time, and see how their top three hitters by WAR stack up against the Rockies' crew. Kris Bryant, Javy Baez and Anthony Rizzo? 67.5 WAR. Justin Turner, Corey Seager and Cody Bellinger? 61.5 WAR. Jose Altuve, George Springer and Alex Bregman? 76.7 WAR.

Are you ready for the horrifying twist? Here it is: All of the hitters who made at least one plate appearance for the Rockies from 2015-2020 and are not named Trevor Story, Nolan Arenado or Charlie Blackmon combined to earn an additional *six wins above replacement*. Six! Apply the same criteria to the Cubs, Dodgers, and Astros and you end up with, respectively, 69.3, 103.1, and 100 additional WAR provided by hitters outside of the team's Top 3.

It seems as if this should not be possible. It is fair to acknowledge the payroll discrepancies that naturally make it harder for Rockies to fill out a productive lineup than it is for the Dodgers, but it also feels fair to say that if you gave any half-decent GM a few million dollars to spend in the free-agent market every year for the last five years, they would be able to cobble together a collection of dudes who could provide more than 6 WAR over the course of a half decade. Bridich has had a lot more than just a few million dollars to spend.

There was the $70 million he splurged on Ian Desmond, the $27.5 million spent on Gerardo Parra and the $24 million that went to Daniel Murphy. Then there was the $24 million not spent on DJ LeMahieu, who fetched that much money from the Yankees in the 2018 offseason and immediately started playing like an MVP candidate.

It gets worse! We must unfortunately revisit Bridich's attempt to imitate the champion 2015 Royals by assembling a super bullpen, which amounted to spending a combined $135 million on Jason Motte, Mike Dunn, Wade Davis, Jake McGee and Bryan Shaw. Add these fellas' contributions to those of the aforementioned crew of free-agent hitters and what do you get? Negative 3.7 WAR. Drew Butera was a better pitcher than they were collectively, even on a rate basis. Like I said, being a Rockies fan is very frustrating.

Some of these missteps could have been corrected with the rise of home-grown talent. The best way to fill a giant hole in your payroll is to develop some studs from the farm system and get a bunch of wins out of them while paying them peanuts. This is another one of those things that good baseball teams tend to be good at, and which the Rockies have been horrifyingly bad at. Unless you are a close observer of the Rockies, it's entirely possible that you have never even heard of Ryan McMahon, Jeff Hoffman, Brendan Rodgers, Jon Gray, Garrett Hampson or Raimel Tapia. That's because none of these players are very good at baseball, despite all having been tabbed at one point or another as potential stars.

Would you like to hear a particularly grim story about just how bad the Rockies are at developing their own talent? Do you remember Tyler Matzek? The Rockies drafted him 11th overall in the 2009 draft, and he came into their system with the stuff and pedigree of a potential ace. During his years with the Rockies, he developed a debilitating case of the yips that robbed him of his ability to throw the ball in anything resembling much of a straight line, and washed out of the sport in 2016. Bad luck for the Rockies, right? Can't do much about a guy getting the yips.

Matzek spent the 2020 season as an anchor in the Atlanta Braves' bullpen, posting a 2.79 ERA in 21 appearances, and striking out 43 batters in 29 innings.

What's to be made of this kind of abject failure at building a baseball team? The impulse is to throw mud, to call Bridich and the rest of the Rockies front office morons for having spent money on players they thought would be good but were actually bad, to sneer and invoke teams like the Oakland A's and Tampa Bay Rays as examples of small-market clubs that actually understand how to find wins on the margins and build contending teams on the fly. And honestly, how can you not laugh at the Rockies spending $135 million on a bullpen full of duds while those other teams were busy figuring out how to get to the World Series by signing all the Jake Diekmans and Aaron Loups of the world for a few bags of pennies? (Even McGee got his ring after being revived by the Dodgers.)

I'd like to offer a different way of looking at the Rockies' most recent failures at roster construction, and to do so by, perversely, borrowing a phrase from the sort of analytics-minded person who would most eagerly scoff at Colorado's efforts: Sometimes the process is more important than the results. Which is to say, it's good when a team with the Rockies' market size and ambition decides to spend money.

Yes, the money Bridich has spent over the last five years has unequivocally been wasted, but the intentions behind those signings were good. Bridich wasn't wrong to identify the bullpen as a thing worth investing in, he was just wrong to think building a good one actually had to cost money. He wasn't wrong to spend money on hitters to pad the lineup around his three stars, he just picked the wrong hitters, guessing the money was better spent on Ian Desmond and Daniel Murphy rather than LeMahieu—who was already a key member of the Rockies' lineup!—and, say, Marcell Ozuna.

Perhaps it seems like I am setting an exceptionally low bar here—after all, it has historically been a GM's job to figure out which players are worth spending money on and which are not—but given recent trends in baseball, it's something of a virtue to be willing to spend any money at all. We're several years into an era in which the free-agent market just gets colder every winter, and what can be charitably described as soft collusion has made it extremely difficult for even the league's best free agents to receive competitive offers for their services.

It feels like we are headed towards a grim future in which every team in the league agrees that there are only two ways to play for a championship: be like the Dodgers or be like the Rays. The few teams that can afford to spend like the Dodgers will go on offering themselves up as landing spots for the very best players in the league; the many teams who will see following Rays' blueprint as a more sensible course of action will continue to squeeze and squeeze and squeeze their payrolls while trying to game their way into a Wild Card spot. This may seem like an alarmist vision of the future, but it's hard to watch teams like Chicago and Cleveland go from being World Series contestants to belt-tighteners within four seasons and not hear sirens. The Reds tried for one year and they're already exhausted.

Now is a time in which the league needs *more* teams like the Rockies, not fewer. If baseball is going to continue to be a sport in which competition matters, in which players can be expected to have their efforts rewarded in an equitable market, then there simply have to be some teams in the league that are willing to slap $70 million on the table for players of Ian Desmond's (apparent) caliber. Or even $7 million, to outbid the smart teams on their non-tendered free agents and dumpster dives.

It's possible to imagine a future in which the Rockies continue to spend like they have over the last half decade *and* actually manage to win some baseball games. There is currently a lot of ground for the taking in baseball's marketplace, just begging to be staked out by a mid-market team that's willing to spend good money in pursuit of wins. The Rockies could be that team, if they were just smarter about how their money gets spent.

The trouble is that being that kind of smart, the kind of smart that isn't synonymous with frugality and arbitrage, is a hard thing to be. If Jeff Bridich knew better than to spend $52 million on Wade Davis, he wouldn't be Jeff Bridich. And if he weren't Jeff Bridich, he'd probably be one of the scores of GMs who have accepted that spending real money on roster construction is a virtue that no longer needs to be bothered with. Which leads us to the worst possible outcome, and the most likely one: A future in which Bridich accepts that the days of free-spending are over, but in which he is just as dense about where money needs to be saved as he has been about where it should be spent.

The first big move the Rockies made this offseason was non-tendering David Dahl instead of paying him $3 million. The 26-year-old outfielder was an All-Star in 2019, and the only player from the team's latest batch of prospects who ever looked, even for a moment, like a potential star. If the Rockies are going to be as unskilled at austerity as they have been at scouting, spending, and development, then things are about to get much, much worse.

—*Tom Ley is a co-owner of Defector.*

Part 2: Player Analysis

PLAYER COMMENTS WITH GRAPHS

Charlie Blackmon RF
Born: 07/01/86   Age: 35   Bats: L   Throws: L
Height: 6'3"   Weight: 221   Origin: Round 2, 2008 Draft (#72 overall)

YEAR	TEAM	LVL	AGE	PA	R	2B	3B	HR	RBI	BB	K	SB	CS	AVG/OBP/SLG
2018	COL	MLB	31	696	119	31	7	29	70	59	134	12	4	.291/.358/.502
2019	COL	MLB	32	634	112	42	7	32	86	40	104	2	5	.314/.364/.576
2020	COL	MLB	33	247	31	12	1	6	42	19	44	2	1	.303/.356/.448
2021 FS	COL	MLB	34	600	83	27	5	23	74	46	121	11	6	.279/.349/.481
2021 DC	COL	MLB	34	578	80	26	5	23	72	44	117	11	5	.279/.349/.481

Comparables: Ellis Burks, Carlos Beltrán, Larry Hisle

Could someone hit .400 in the short season? Blackmon gave it the college try, registering .406 at nearly the halfway mark (and even hitting .500 through 17 games) before parachuting with a line around .200 the rest of the way to finish 19th overall. It wasn't as prodigious a quest as Todd Helton's two decades prior (though both were in great position in mid-August, a tremendous feat when freed of any other context). Batting race aside, age snuck up on Blackmon and his densely-hedged chin; at this point, most of his productivity is the result of making good but not monstrous contact. So in a way, he's forever locked in a batting average race.

YEAR	TEAM	LVL	AGE	PA	DRC+	BABIP	BRR	FRAA	WARP
2018	COL	MLB	31	696	122	.329	-0.6	CF(151): -21.7	2.1
2019	COL	MLB	32	634	129	.334	0.4	RF(135): -8.8	3.0
2020	COL	MLB	33	247	115	.347	1.0	RF(50): -0.2	1.2
2021 FS	COL	MLB	34	600	122	.326	1.0	RF -1, CF 0	3.3
2021 DC	COL	MLB	34	578	122	.326	1.0	RF -1	2.8

Charlie Blackmon, continued

Batted Ball Distribution

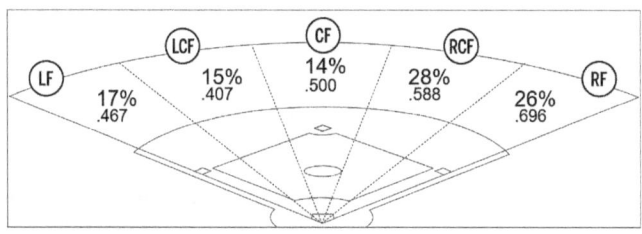

Strike Zone vs LHP   Strike Zone vs RHP

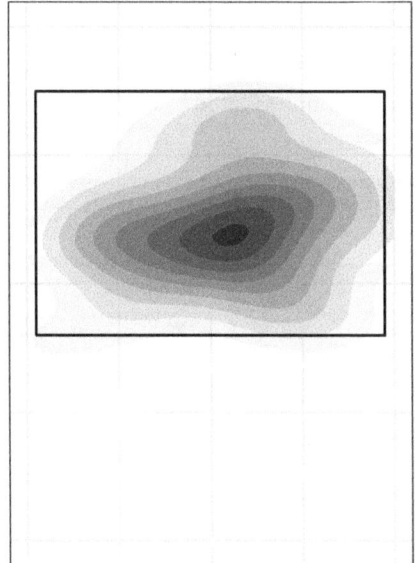
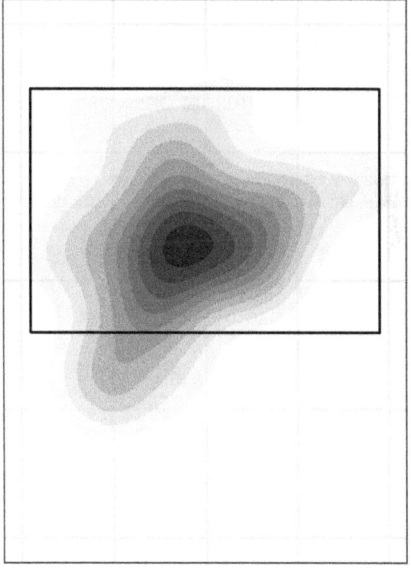

Colorado Rockies 2021

Elias Díaz C

Born: 11/17/90   Age: 30   Bats: R   Throws: R
Height: 6'1"   Weight: 223   Origin: International Free Agent, 2008

YEAR	TEAM	LVL	AGE	PA	R	2B	3B	HR	RBI	BB	K	SB	CS	AVG/OBP/SLG
2018	PIT	MLB	27	277	33	12	0	10	34	21	40	0	1	.286/.339/.452
2019	IND	AAA	28	30	5	3	0	0	4	1	5	0	0	.414/.433/.517
2019	PIT	MLB	28	332	31	14	0	2	28	23	55	0	0	.241/.296/.307
2020	COL	MLB	29	73	4	2	0	2	9	5	15	0	0	.235/.288/.353
2021 FS	COL	MLB	30	600	61	25	1	13	59	41	121	1	1	.245/.302/.371
2021 DC	COL	MLB	30	391	39	16	1	8	38	27	78	0	1	.245/.302/.371

Comparables: Vance Wilson, Dick Billings, Brook Fordyce

A year after being identified as the poorest framer in the entire league, Díaz figured, shoot, if he can't steal strike three, he might as well go to the pitching staff that allows the most balls in play. Clever transaction. As a backup he carried the Rockies catching crew from a power perspective, being the only one of the lot who cleared the outfield wall at least once. He can "run into one", as they like to say, about as often as he can frame into one.

YEAR	TEAM	P. COUNT	FRM RUNS	BLK RUNS	THRW RUNS	TOT RUNS
2018	PIT	9208	-1.2	-2.0	0.1	-3.1
2019	PIT	12603	-14.4	0.1	-0.1	-14.4
2020	COL	2173	0.3	-0.2	0.0	0.1
2021	COL	15632	-5.7	0.1	-0.5	-6.1
2021	COL	15632	-5.7	-1.5	-0.5	-7.7

YEAR	TEAM	LVL	AGE	PA	DRC+	BABIP	BRR	FRAA	WARP
2018	PIT	MLB	27	277	112	.302	0.5	C(70): 0.6	1.9
2019	IND	AAA	28	30	117	.500	0.0	C(6): 0.7	0.2
2019	PIT	MLB	28	332	72	.285	1.3	C(96): -11.0	-0.4
2020	COL	MLB	29	73	87	.275	0.2	C(24): -0.0	0.1
2021 FS	COL	MLB	30	600	82	.293	-0.7	C -5	0.5
2021 DC	COL	MLB	30	391	82	.293	-0.5	C -5	0.2

Elias Díaz, continued

Batted Ball Distribution

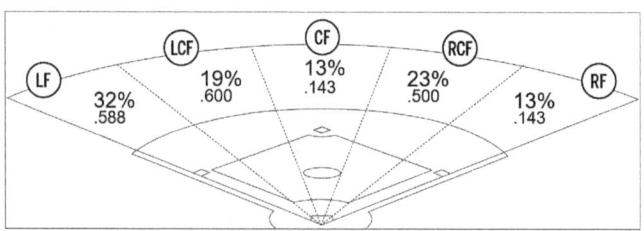

Strike Zone vs LHP　　　**Strike Zone vs RHP**

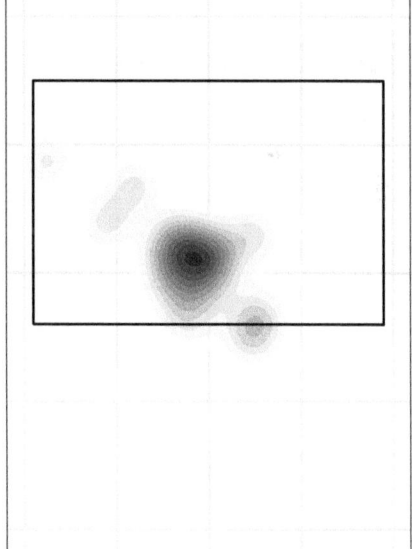

Colorado Rockies 2021

Josh Fuentes 3B

Born: 02/19/93   Age: 28   Bats: R   Throws: R
Height: 6'2"   Weight: 209   Origin: Undrafted Free Agent, 2014

YEAR	TEAM	LVL	AGE	PA	R	2B	3B	HR	RBI	BB	K	SB	CS	AVG/OBP/SLG
2018	ABQ	AAA	25	586	93	39	12	14	95	21	103	3	5	.327/.354/.517
2019	ABQ	AAA	26	437	66	23	2	17	64	25	118	1	1	.254/.298/.448
2019	COL	MLB	26	56	8	1	0	3	7	1	20	1	0	.218/.232/.400
2020	COL	MLB	27	103	14	7	0	2	17	2	29	1	0	.306/.320/.439
2021 FS	COL	MLB	28	600	63	24	5	18	69	25	170	1	1	.240/.285/.402
2021 DC	COL	MLB	28	218	23	8	2	6	25	9	61	0	1	.240/.285/.402

Comparables: Will Middlebrooks, Chris Johnson, Matt Macri

   WalkScore.com recently rated Denver as America's 16th walkable city, making it "somewhat walkable. Some errands can be accomplished on foot." It would have ranked higher but Fuentes got a chunk of playing time, and both of his walks were on four straight pitches. For all the cuts, he comes out with a modest average and immodest strikeout rate. He'll need more than that to see more action, either at first base or backing up his cousin Nolan Arenado at third. Otherwise he's not long for the roster, and knowing him, he'll take the train.

YEAR	TEAM	LVL	AGE	PA	DRC+	BABIP	BRR	FRAA	WARP
2018	ABQ	AAA	25	586	109	.376	2.5	3B(110): 6.2, 1B(21): 0.6, 2B(1): 0.3	2.7
2019	ABQ	AAA	26	437	66	.314	0.2	3B(96): 10.3, 1B(1): -0.1, 2B(1): -0.0	0.8
2019	COL	MLB	26	56	72	.281	0.1	1B(11): -0.3, 3B(2): -0.0	-0.1
2020	COL	MLB	27	103	79	.406	0.2	1B(26): 4.4, 3B(6): -0.5, LF(2): -0.0	0.3
2021 FS	COL	MLB	28	600	81	.313	-0.1	1B 3, 2B 0	-0.1
2021 DC	COL	MLB	28	218	81	.313	0.0	1B 1	-0.1

Josh Fuentes, continued

Batted Ball Distribution

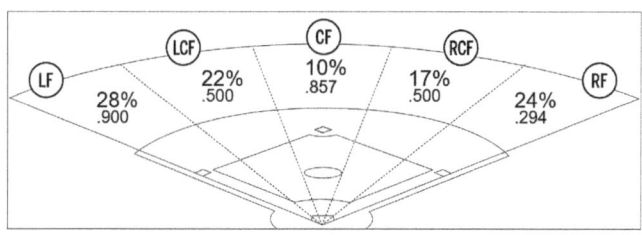

Strike Zone vs LHP   **Strike Zone vs RHP**

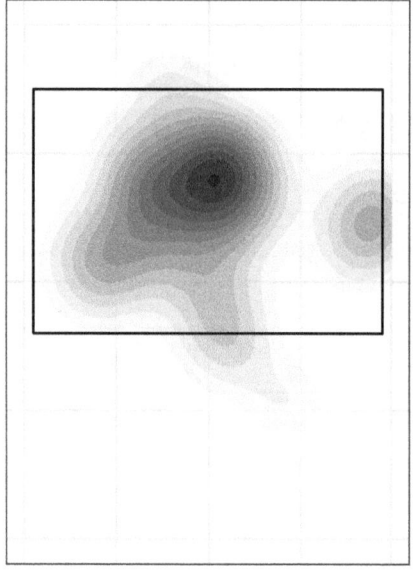

Colorado Rockies 2021

Garrett Hampson 2B

Born: 10/10/94 Age: 26 Bats: R Throws: R
Height: 5'11" Weight: 196 Origin: Round 3, 2016 Draft (#81 overall)

YEAR	TEAM	LVL	AGE	PA	R	2B	3B	HR	RBI	BB	K	SB	CS	AVG/OBP/SLG
2018	HFD	AA	23	172	28	8	2	4	15	21	17	19	1	.304/.391/.466
2018	ABQ	AAA	23	332	53	17	4	6	25	30	58	17	4	.314/.377/.459
2018	COL	MLB	23	48	3	3	1	0	4	7	12	2	0	.275/.396/.400
2019	ABQ	AAA	24	117	15	9	1	2	9	5	25	7	2	.266/.310/.422
2019	COL	MLB	24	327	40	9	4	8	27	24	88	15	3	.247/.302/.385
2020	COL	MLB	25	184	25	4	3	5	11	13	60	6	1	.234/.287/.383
2021 FS	COL	MLB	26	600	67	19	8	14	56	48	174	24	7	.233/.300/.377
2021 DC	COL	MLB	26	541	61	17	7	13	51	43	156	22	6	.233/.300/.377

Comparables: Jerry Buchek, Roberto Mejia, Bobby Hill

    Speed is somewhat of a cursed tool with baseball players; it defines you more than the other four, perhaps because it's the one that cannot be learned. When development is a priority, a slow slugger will always get more playing time than a speedy slapper. By sprint speed, Hampson is one of the 10 fastest runners in the league. It helps that he can play infield and outfield, but the lagging bat makes him a perfect pinch runner/fourth outfielder. Having said that about his swinging struggles, he *is* the first guy to homer twice in a 23-5 loss.

YEAR	TEAM	LVL	AGE	PA	DRC+	BABIP	BRR	FRAA	WARP
2018	HFD	AA	23	172	135	.323	3.5	SS(18): 0.4, 2B(17): 1.7, CF(3): -0.1	1.6
2018	ABQ	AAA	23	332	109	.372	0.9	2B(44): -0.1, SS(23): -2.3, CF(6): 1.4	1.1
2018	COL	MLB	23	48	81	.393	1.1	SS(8): 0.2, 2B(7): 0.6, CF(1): -0.1	0.2
2019	ABQ	AAA	24	117	63	.329	1.0	2B(15): 0.3, SS(10): -1.5	-0.1
2019	COL	MLB	24	327	70	.322	3.5	2B(50): -1.1, CF(31): -0.8, SS(15): -0.1	0.1
2020	COL	MLB	25	184	72	.330	2.0	2B(26): -1.8, CF(20): -2.2, LF(7): 0.0	-0.4
2021 FS	COL	MLB	26	600	81	.318	3.1	CF 0, 2B 0	0.6
2021 DC	COL	MLB	26	541	81	.318	2.8	CF 0, 2B 0	0.5

Garrett Hampson, continued

Batted Ball Distribution

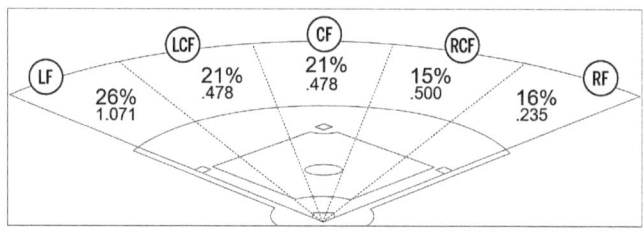

Strike Zone vs LHP   Strike Zone vs RHP

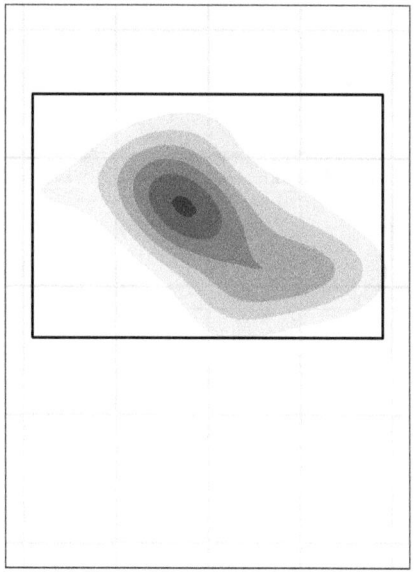

Colorado Rockies 2021

Sam Hilliard   RF
Born: 02/21/94   Age: 27   Bats: L   Throws: L
Height: 6'5"   Weight: 236   Origin: Round 15, 2015 Draft (#437 overall)

YEAR	TEAM	LVL	AGE	PA	R	2B	3B	HR	RBI	BB	K	SB	CS	AVG/OBP/SLG
2018	HFD	AA	24	484	58	22	3	9	40	41	151	23	14	.262/.327/.389
2019	ABQ	AAA	25	559	109	29	7	35	101	54	164	22	5	.262/.335/.558
2019	COL	MLB	25	87	13	4	2	7	13	9	23	2	0	.273/.356/.649
2020	COL	MLB	26	114	13	2	2	6	10	9	42	3	0	.210/.272/.438
2021 FS	COL	MLB	27	600	66	24	6	18	65	48	215	15	7	.221/.290/.389
2021 DC	COL	MLB	27	515	56	21	5	16	56	41	185	13	6	.221/.290/.389

Comparables: Carlos Peguero, Curtis Granderson, Daniel Palka

There's a theory going around that all Rockies outfielders are nothing more than mild derivatives of Larry Walker, the ur-Rockies outfielder. Hilliard has the speed and the power but lacks the swing to leverage either. The breakout year in Albuquerque was almost certainly inflated, as more mature pitching kept him fishing for big game and winding up with nothing but boot after flavorless boot. Despite that—and admittedly it was a lean year for dingers in Colorado—he had the team's finest ratio of HR/PA. With that in mind, conking baseballs into bleachers forgives most other on-field transgressions, so the potential for home runs will tempt Bud Black into giving him playing time over the rest of the Walkerlings.

YEAR	TEAM	LVL	AGE	PA	DRC+	BABIP	BRR	FRAA	WARP
2018	HFD	AA	24	484	97	.379	0.3	RF(70): 3.5, LF(29): -1.8, CF(12): -0.5	0.3
2019	ABQ	AAA	25	559	98	.316	0.5	RF(83): -0.2, CF(34): 5.2, LF(10): -0.6	1.8
2019	COL	MLB	25	87	108	.298	0.7	CF(17): 0.6, RF(6): 1.7, LF(5): -1.2	0.5
2020	COL	MLB	26	114	70	.281	1.0	LF(14): 3.2, RF(13): 0.2, CF(10): -0.4	0.3
2021 FS	COL	MLB	27	600	79	.331	1.9	CF 2, RF 1	0.4
2021 DC	COL	MLB	27	515	79	.331	1.6	CF 2, RF 1	0.4

Sam Hilliard, continued

Batted Ball Distribution

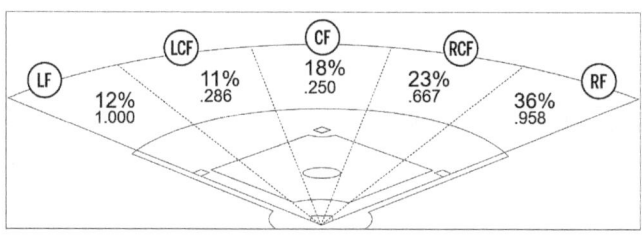

Strike Zone vs LHP   Strike Zone vs RHP

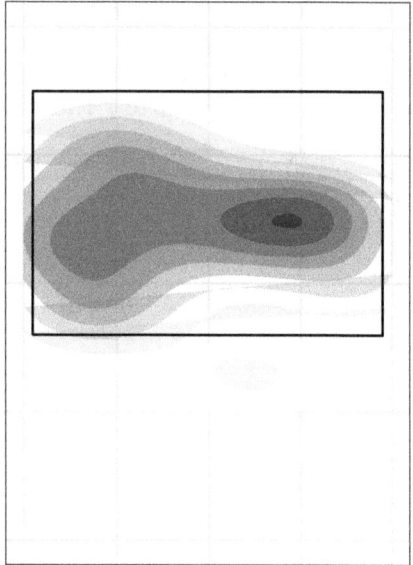

Matt Kemp LF

Born: 09/23/84   Age: 36   Bats: R   Throws: R
Height: 6'4"   Weight: 225   Origin: Round 6, 2003 Draft (#181 overall)

YEAR	TEAM	LVL	AGE	PA	R	2B	3B	HR	RBI	BB	K	SB	CS	AVG/OBP/SLG
2018	LAD	MLB	33	506	62	25	0	21	85	36	115	0	0	.290/.338/.481
2019	SYR	AAA	34	36	3	0	0	1	3	2	7	0	0	.235/.278/.324
2019	CIN	MLB	34	62	4	2	0	1	5	1	19	0	0	.200/.210/.283
2020	COL	MLB	35	132	18	3	0	6	21	15	41	1	0	.239/.326/.419
2021 FS	COL	MLB	36	600	64	19	1	24	74	40	177	1	1	.223/.280/.391

Comparables: Andruw Jones, Dale Murphy, Carl Everett

Most National League fans love themselves some hittin' pitchers. There's a smaller share who don't mind if the DH permeates both leagues, and within that, a niche who absolutely want it, and a subset within that niche that is just Kemp himself, desparately depending on it. The former star center fielder has diminished bat speed and is primarily a platoon bench player, at this point which means his playing time goes up if all 30 teams ban their pitcher from wearing a helmet. Kemp and his degenerative hip managed to stay productive for a very long time, if less so over the last two years, spanning four organizations. He seems content living the organized sporting life and the teams seem content handing him a uniform with his name on it; maybe he'll hang around just long enough to DH his way to 300 career home runs.

YEAR	TEAM	LVL	AGE	PA	DRC+	BABIP	BRR	FRAA	WARP
2018	LAD	MLB	33	506	115	.339	-2.1	LF(75): -1.5, RF(51): -2.2	1.6
2019	SYR	AAA	34	36	71	.269	-0.5	LF(3): -0.7	-0.2
2019	CIN	MLB	34	62	72	.268	0.0	LF(17): -1.6	-0.2
2020	COL	MLB	35	132	91	.314	0.3	LF(1): 0.1	0.2
2021 FS	COL	MLB	36	600	77	.283	-0.8	LF -1, RF -6	-1.2

Matt Kemp, continued

Batted Ball Distribution

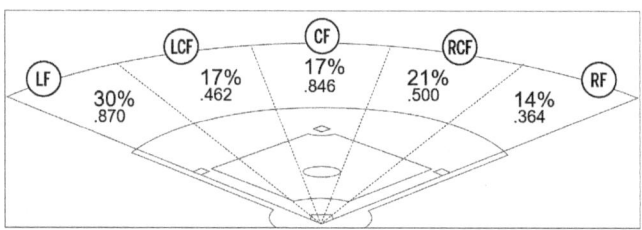

Strike Zone vs LHP   **Strike Zone vs RHP**

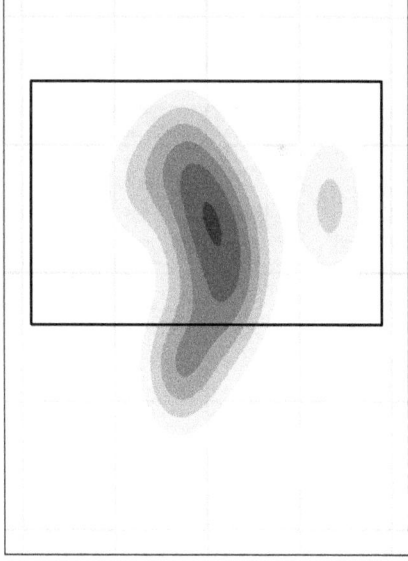

Colorado Rockies 2021

Ryan McMahon 2B
Born: 12/14/94 Age: 26 Bats: L Throws: R
Height: 6'2" Weight: 219 Origin: Round 2, 2013 Draft (#42 overall)

YEAR	TEAM	LVL	AGE	PA	R	2B	3B	HR	RBI	BB	K	SB	CS	AVG/OBP/SLG
2018	ABQ	AAA	23	242	40	15	3	11	48	15	61	3	2	.290/.339/.531
2018	COL	MLB	23	202	17	9	1	5	19	18	64	1	0	.232/.307/.376
2019	COL	MLB	24	539	70	22	1	24	83	56	160	5	1	.250/.329/.450
2020	COL	MLB	25	193	23	6	1	9	26	18	66	0	1	.215/.295/.419
2021 FS	COL	MLB	26	600	72	20	3	26	77	54	197	2	2	.230/.307/.427
2021 DC	COL	MLB	26	527	63	18	3	23	67	47	173	2	2	.230/.307/.427

Comparables: Danny Espinosa, Mark Bellhorn, Jared Sandberg

There is something endearing about a baseballer with incredible power, but without the ability to wield it. Sure, A-Rod, Pujols and Cabrera were able to bop seemingly at will. The McMahons of the league can "make that sound" when they strike the bad pitch correctly, and they do that nearly enough, but when the dust settles on the season, we're left with a collection of homers and a larger collection of nothing. It's part and parcel of the player's allure and humanity: They do one thing extremely well, but only sometimes, and that's completely relatable. We're all rooting for that random season where he scrapes a .220 average and belts 40 beyond the walls.

YEAR	TEAM	LVL	AGE	PA	DRC+	BABIP	BRR	FRAA	WARP
2018	ABQ	AAA	23	242	106	.353	1.9	1B(43): -1.9, 2B(10): -1.0, 3B(2): -0.3	0.2
2018	COL	MLB	23	202	74	.327	0.9	1B(31): -1.1, 3B(17): 0.1, 2B(10): 0.9	-0.1
2019	COL	MLB	24	539	92	.323	-0.1	2B(113): 6.9, 3B(22): -0.5, 1B(19): -0.6	1.7
2020	COL	MLB	25	193	85	.286	0.2	2B(33): -0.5, 3B(14): 2.7, 1B(12): 0.8	0.5
2021 FS	COL	MLB	26	600	95	.312	-0.1	3B 1, 2B 0	1.2
2021 DC	COL	MLB	26	527	95	.312	-0.1	3B 1, 2B 0	0.9

Ryan McMahon, continued

Batted Ball Distribution

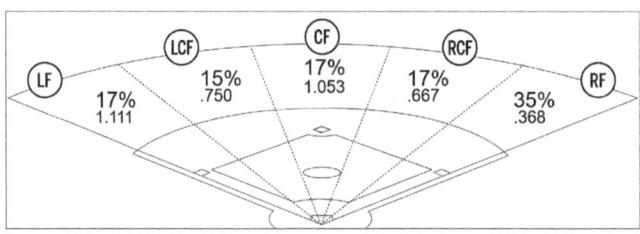

Strike Zone vs LHP   Strike Zone vs RHP

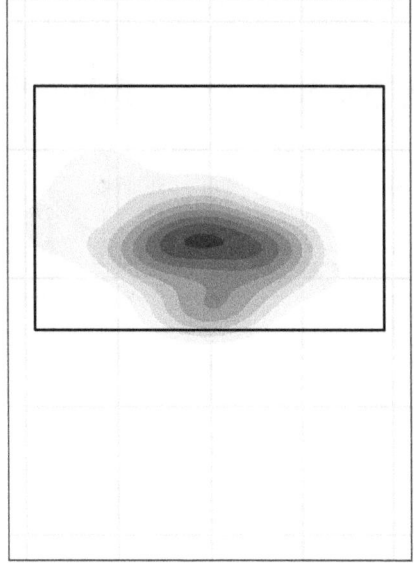

Colorado Rockies 2021

Daniel Murphy 1B

Born: 04/01/85 Age: 36 Bats: L Throws: R
Height: 6'1" Weight: 223 Origin: Round 13, 2006 Draft (#394 overall)

YEAR	TEAM	LVL	AGE	PA	R	2B	3B	HR	RBI	BB	K	SB	CS	AVG/OBP/SLG
2018	HBG	AA	33	44	8	2	0	2	7	6	4	0	0	.243/.364/.459
2018	WAS	MLB	33	205	17	9	0	6	29	13	17	1	0	.300/.341/.442
2018	CHC	MLB	33	146	23	6	0	6	13	7	23	2	0	.297/.329/.471
2019	COL	MLB	34	478	56	35	1	13	78	32	74	1	1	.279/.328/.452
2020	COL	MLB	35	132	10	3	0	3	16	7	21	0	0	.236/.275/.333
2021 FS	COL	MLB	36	600	64	28	2	17	70	41	94	3	2	.263/.321/.421

Comparables: Aaron Hill, Carlos Baerga, Brandon Phillips

    A career dud year at age 35 made it a fairly simple decision for the Rockies to say no to another year of *that* for $12 million. He clearly succumbed to Chronic Second Baseman Dystrophy, better known outside the medical world as Dan Uggla Syndrome. This usually happens to folk in their mid 30s, and there's no known cure. He tried to hide it by playing a lot of first base, but you can't fool anyone. It follows you. Plenty have tried. Having an NLCS MVP in his trophy case could give him another year or so to hang around a team and pinch hit if he chooses, because avoiding strikeouts is his only party trick left.

YEAR	TEAM	LVL	AGE	PA	DRC+	BABIP	BRR	FRAA	WARP
2018	HBG	AA	33	44	120	.226	0.5	2B(8): -0.6, 1B(2): 0.3	0.2
2018	WAS	MLB	33	205	114	.302	-1.0	2B(38): -2.9, 1B(14): -0.6	0.4
2018	CHC	MLB	33	146	111	.318	0.7	2B(33): -1.1	0.6
2019	COL	MLB	34	478	97	.307	0.0	1B(110): 5.9, 2B(3): 0.4	1.2
2020	COL	MLB	35	132	90	.260	-1.7	1B(29): 0.1	0.0
2021 FS	COL	MLB	36	600	98	.292	-0.4	1B 1, 2B -2	0.9

Daniel Murphy, continued

Batted Ball Distribution

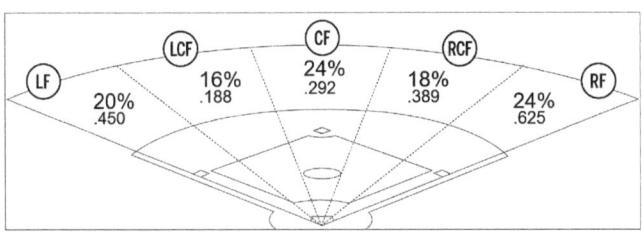

Strike Zone vs LHP   **Strike Zone vs RHP**

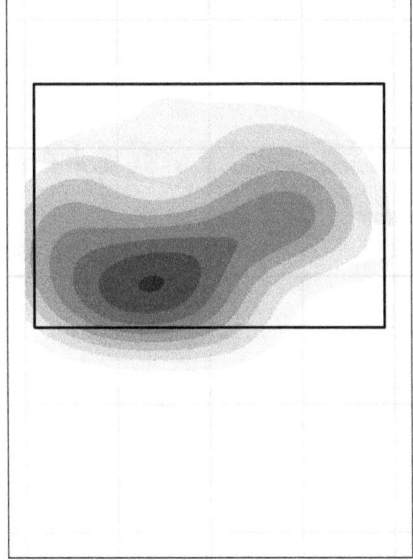

Colorado Rockies 2021

Chris Owings SS
Born: 08/12/91   Age: 29   Bats: R   Throws: R
Height: 5'10"   Weight: 185   Origin: Round 1, 2009 Draft (#41 overall)

YEAR	TEAM	LVL	AGE	PA	R	2B	3B	HR	RBI	BB	K	SB	CS	AVG/OBP/SLG
2018	RNO	AAA	26	92	15	4	2	1	11	1	17	1	2	.286/.293/.407
2018	ARI	MLB	26	309	34	15	0	4	22	24	75	11	4	.206/.272/.302
2019	WOR	AAA	27	183	26	11	0	11	34	15	50	6	4	.325/.385/.595
2019	BOS	MLB	27	51	4	2	0	1	5	6	23	1	1	.156/.255/.267
2019	KC	MLB	27	145	9	4	1	2	9	8	55	4	1	.133/.193/.222
2020	COL	MLB	28	44	9	1	0	2	5	3	11	1	0	.268/.318/.439
2021 FS	COL	MLB	29	600	57	23	3	16	64	36	165	16	5	.224/.279/.369

Comparables: Alex Gonzalez, Josh Rutledge, Greg Gagne

Having already endured two nadirs before his 28th birthday, there was nowhere for Owings but to go up. Even retiring from baseball would be somewhat of a relief. No more getting roasted by the fellas at the batter's box. No more two-week road trips. No more "talk about" reporter questions. Perhaps plenty of fresh air on a farm, or maybe by the ocean? Mess around with watercolors? Check out the farmers' market? But with him being relatively young, Owings opted for more baseball and held his own. It was technically a career high by OPS, but it was also technically a month in Colorado. He's a utility player with chaotic production, what's not to love?

YEAR	TEAM	LVL	AGE	PA	DRC+	BABIP	BRR	FRAA	WARP
2018	RNO	AAA	26	92	64	.342	1.4	2B(10): -0.2, 3B(6): 0.3, CF(3): -0.4	0.0
2018	ARI	MLB	26	309	69	.265	0.8	RF(43): -1.1, CF(16): 1.2, 3B(15): -0.8	-0.4
2019	WOR	AAA	27	183	140	.404	-1.0	SS(18): 0.3, 2B(10): 1.5, 3B(6): -0.3	1.4
2019	BOS	MLB	27	51	29	.286	-1.0	2B(12): 0.2, SS(7): 0.7, 3B(1): -0.0	-0.3
2019	KC	MLB	27	145	34	.205	0.9	2B(13): -1.8, 3B(12): 1.4, CF(7): -0.2	-0.7
2020	COL	MLB	28	44	100	.321	0.4	2B(8): -0.3, 3B(2): -0.2, LF(2): -0.1	0.1
2021 FS	COL	MLB	29	600	72	.290	1.4	2B 0, RF 0	-0.4

Chris Owings, continued

Batted Ball Distribution

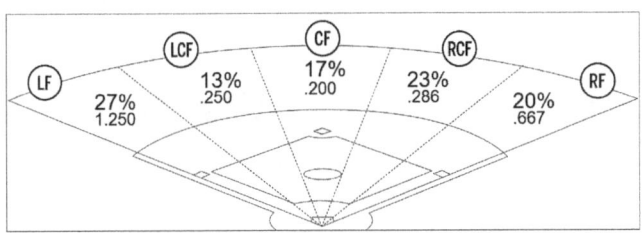

Strike Zone vs LHP   Strike Zone vs RHP

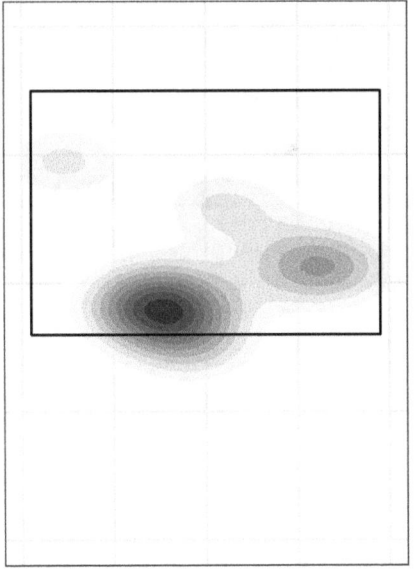

Colorado Rockies 2021

Kevin Pillar CF
Born: 01/04/89 Age: 32 Bats: R Throws: R
Height: 6'0" Weight: 200 Origin: Round 32, 2011 Draft (#979 overall)

YEAR	TEAM	LVL	AGE	PA	R	2B	3B	HR	RBI	BB	K	SB	CS	AVG/OBP/SLG
2018	TOR	MLB	29	542	65	40	2	15	59	18	98	14	3	.252/.282/.426
2019	TOR	MLB	30	17	1	0	0	0	1	0	3	0	0	.062/.059/.062
2019	SF	MLB	30	628	82	37	3	21	87	18	86	14	5	.264/.293/.442
2020	COL	MLB	31	97	14	5	1	2	13	5	18	4	1	.308/.351/.451
2020	BOS	MLB	31	126	20	7	2	4	13	8	23	1	1	.274/.325/.470
2021 FS	COL	MLB	32	600	60	29	2	18	69	28	113	14	6	.247/.291/.404
2021 DC	COL	MLB	32	274	27	13	1	8	31	12	51	6	3	.247/.291/.404

Comparables: Henry Cotto, Tsuyoshi Shinjo, Gerald Williams

Corinthian to the core, Pillar is going to get his share of home runs because he's contact-prone and swings upward. In 2019 he became the fourth San Francisco center fielder to sock at least 20 in a season (Marquis Grissom, Chili Davis and someone named Mays are the others). That consistency made him ideal trade deadline fodder for the sinking Red Sox, assuming you can call what Colorado did a playoff push. The existence of power and presence of batting average, coupled with extra-base speed and range, gives Pillar the bare minimum of everything you want in a center fielder. Aging into his 30s doesn't give the team much more than the low-ceiling skill set, but you can't hold up a ceiling without a pillar.

YEAR	TEAM	LVL	AGE	PA	DRC+	BABIP	BRR	FRAA	WARP
2018	TOR	MLB	29	542	93	.281	3.3	CF(142): 9.0	2.8
2019	TOR	MLB	30	17	26	.071	0.0	CF(4): 0.1	-0.1
2019	SF	MLB	30	628	86	.275	4.1	CF(129): -10.8, RF(27): 0.2	0.4
2020	COL	MLB	31	97	105	.366	1.0	CF(21): -3.1, RF(1): -0.1	0.2
2020	BOS	MLB	31	126	108	.311	1.3	RF(24): -1.5, CF(6): 0.7, LF(2): 0.3	0.6
2021 FS	COL	MLB	32	600	87	.280	1.0	CF 2, RF 0	1.4
2021 DC	COL	MLB	32	274	87	.280	0.4	CF 1, RF 0	0.6

Kevin Pillar, continued

Batted Ball Distribution

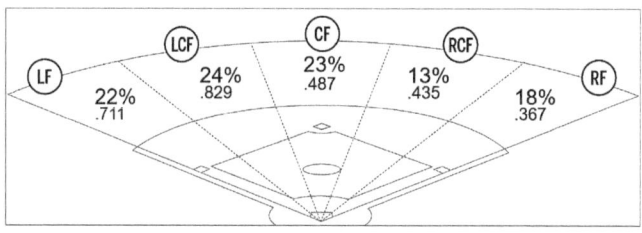

Strike Zone vs LHP   Strike Zone vs RHP

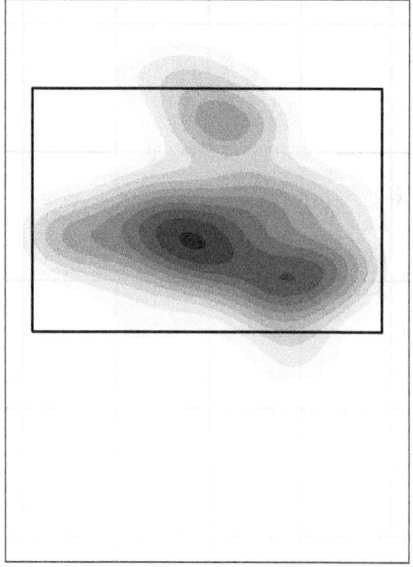

Colorado Rockies 2021

Trevor Story SS
Born: 11/15/92 Age: 28 Bats: R Throws: R
Height: 6'2" Weight: 213 Origin: Round 1, 2011 Draft (#45 overall)

YEAR	TEAM	LVL	AGE	PA	R	2B	3B	HR	RBI	BB	K	SB	CS	AVG/OBP/SLG
2018	COL	MLB	25	656	88	42	6	37	108	47	168	27	6	.291/.348/.567
2019	COL	MLB	26	656	111	38	5	35	85	58	174	23	8	.294/.363/.554
2020	COL	MLB	27	259	41	13	4	11	28	24	63	15	3	.289/.355/.519
2021 FS	COL	MLB	28	600	88	26	5	32	81	53	169	16	6	.265/.340/.515
2021 DC	COL	MLB	28	584	86	25	5	31	78	52	164	15	6	.265/.340/.515

Comparables: Mark Reynolds, Javier Báez, Matt Chapman

It wouldn't be rude to look back and declare that Colorado held the most coveted left side of any infield of the last half-decade, a tandem easy to overlook when their team has won a total of one postseason match. Story, who replaced Troy Tulowitzki more seamlessly than anyone imagined, is basically Francisco Lindor minus the glove. That's not to say he can't field; he can, it's just that he's young and athletic enough to spearhead shortstop for now. Among this generation's shortstops he's at the top of the class in home runs and stolen bases, though he's one of the worst at swingin' and missin'. He's a top-tier shortstop, perhaps the most prized of baseball archetypes, and while his team's (lack of) success isn't his fault, that type of player only means good things for your fantasy team.

YEAR	TEAM	LVL	AGE	PA	DRC+	BABIP	BRR	FRAA	WARP
2018	COL	MLB	25	656	127	.345	-0.8	SS(156): -2.0	5.0
2019	COL	MLB	26	656	117	.361	3.5	SS(144): -0.3	4.9
2020	COL	MLB	27	259	125	.354	0.6	SS(57): 0.5	1.5
2021 FS	COL	MLB	28	600	125	.330	1.6	SS 0	3.9
2021 DC	COL	MLB	28	584	125	.330	1.5	SS 0	3.8

Trevor Story, continued

Batted Ball Distribution

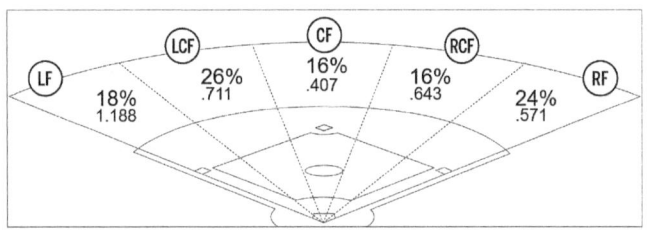

Strike Zone vs LHP   Strike Zone vs RHP

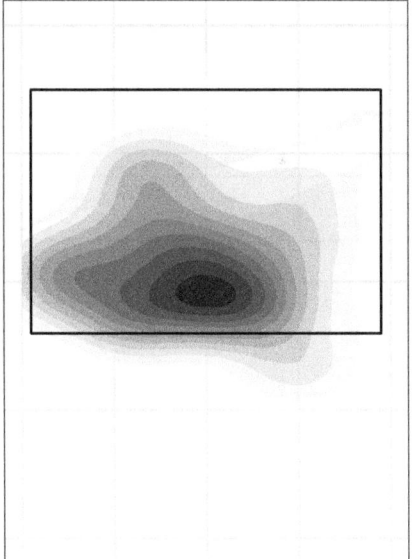

Colorado Rockies 2021

Raimel Tapia LF
Born: 02/04/94 Age: 27 Bats: L Throws: L
Height: 6'3" Weight: 175 Origin: International Free Agent, 2010

YEAR	TEAM	LVL	AGE	PA	R	2B	3B	HR	RBI	BB	K	SB	CS	AVG/OBP/SLG
2018	ABQ	AAA	24	473	81	33	9	11	62	32	85	21	3	.302/.352/.495
2018	COL	MLB	24	27	6	2	1	1	6	2	7	0	0	.200/.259/.480
2019	COL	MLB	25	447	54	23	5	9	44	21	100	9	3	.275/.309/.415
2020	COL	MLB	26	206	26	8	2	1	17	14	38	8	2	.321/.369/.402
2021 FS	COL	MLB	27	600	71	28	8	11	56	34	131	12	5	.266/.317/.406
2021 DC	COL	MLB	27	505	59	24	6	9	47	29	110	10	4	.266/.317/.406

Comparables: Brian Lesher, Mark Brouhard, Todd Hollandsworth

He smacks the ball on the ground and runs for average, making Tapia a perfect leadoff hitter if the year is 1989. His breakout average in the short season still didn't help him in DRC's eyes, because the lion's share of those hits were singles. You'd expect a fast leadoff dude to bring in a few more doubles, or even cover more ground in left field. We knew Harold Reynolds, we watched Harold Reynolds, and you, sir, are no Harold Reynolds.

YEAR	TEAM	LVL	AGE	PA	DRC+	BABIP	BRR	FRAA	WARP
2018	ABQ	AAA	24	473	99	.354	1.4	CF(65): -5.2, RF(24): -0.0, LF(15): -2.2	0.2
2018	COL	MLB	24	27	87	.235	0.7	CF(6): -0.4, LF(1): -0.0, RF(1): -0.0	0.1
2019	COL	MLB	25	447	79	.341	-0.4	LF(91): 1.7, CF(13): -0.4, RF(6): -0.6	0.1
2020	COL	MLB	26	206	83	.392	1.8	LF(36): -2.0, RF(3): -0.4	-0.1
2021 FS	COL	MLB	27	600	92	.334	1.4	LF 1, CF 0	1.2
2021 DC	COL	MLB	27	505	92	.334	1.2	LF 0	0.8

Raimel Tapia, continued

Batted Ball Distribution

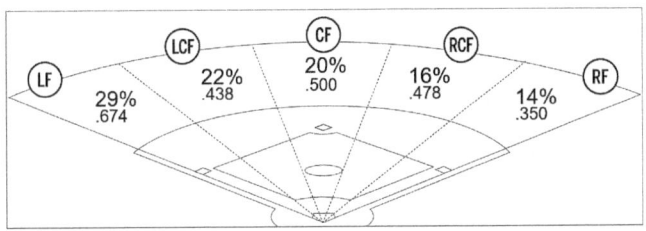

Strike Zone vs LHP

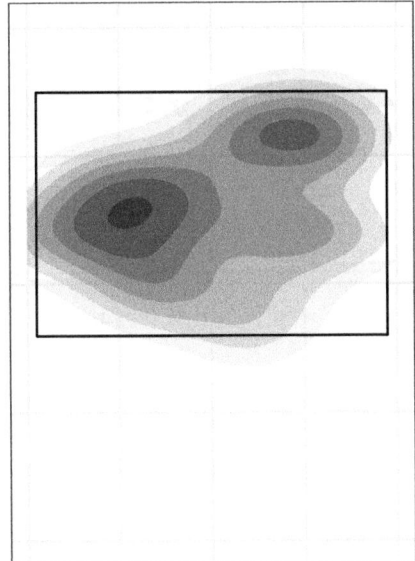

Strike Zone vs RHP

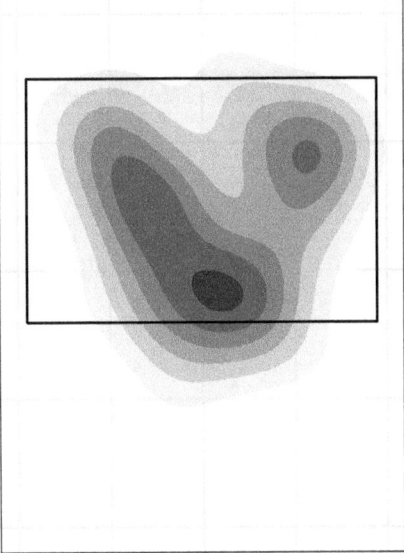

Yency Almonte   RHP

Born: 06/04/94   Age: 27   Bats: S   Throws: R
Height: 6'5"   Weight: 223   Origin: Round 17, 2012 Draft (#537 overall)

YEAR	TEAM	LVL	AGE	W	L	SV	G	GS	IP	H	HR	BB/9	K/9	K	GB%	BABIP
2018	ABQ	AAA	24	3	5	1	18	10	43^2	44	8	2.9	7.0	34	42.2%	.293
2018	COL	MLB	24	0	0	0	14	0	14^2	15	1	2.5	8.6	14	45.2%	.341
2019	ABQ	AAA	25	2	3	5	30	0	30	29	2	7.8	9.6	32	49.4%	.318
2019	COL	MLB	25	0	1	0	28	0	34	39	7	3.7	7.7	29	32.7%	.305
2020	COL	MLB	26	3	0	1	24	0	27^2	25	2	2.0	7.5	23	55.6%	.291
2021 FS	COL	MLB	27	2	3	0	57	0	50	48	7	4.3	8.1	44	44.9%	.289
2021 DC	COL	MLB	27	2	2	0	49	0	52.3	50	8	4.3	8.1	47	44.9%	.289

Comparables: Chase De Jong, Drew Anderson, Jorge López

Trying to make the Rockies' staff out of groundball pitchers is the equivalent of making the entire plane out of the black box. And yet, Almonte was the rare reliever to avert mayday in the Colorado bullpen, thanks to a four-seamer that wound up on the ground and a slider that wound up in the catcher's mitt. Two-pitch dandies are everywhere in the league, but Almonte started tossing in a changeup with the hopes of moving into the rotation someday. The opportunity hasn't come yet, but controlling air traffic late in games isn't a bad gig either.

YEAR	TEAM	LVL	AGE	WHIP	ERA	DRA-	WARP	MPH	FB%	WHF	CSP
2018	ABQ	AAA	24	1.33	5.56	97	0.5				
2018	COL	MLB	24	1.30	1.84	97	0.1	97.0	62.9%	26.0%	
2019	ABQ	AAA	25	1.83	4.20	100	0.4				
2019	COL	MLB	25	1.56	5.56	131	-0.4	97.5	56.8%	24.7%	
2020	COL	MLB	26	1.12	2.93	82	0.5	96.8	42.8%	28.1%	
2021 FS	COL	MLB	27	1.44	4.83	105	0.1	97.1	50.7%	26.4%	44.5%
2021 DC	COL	MLB	27	1.44	4.83	105	0.1	97.1	50.7%	26.4%	44.5%

Yency Almonte, continued

Pitch Shape vs LHH

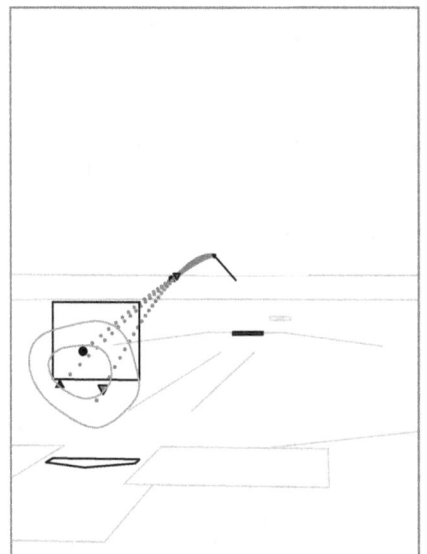

Pitch Shape vs RHH

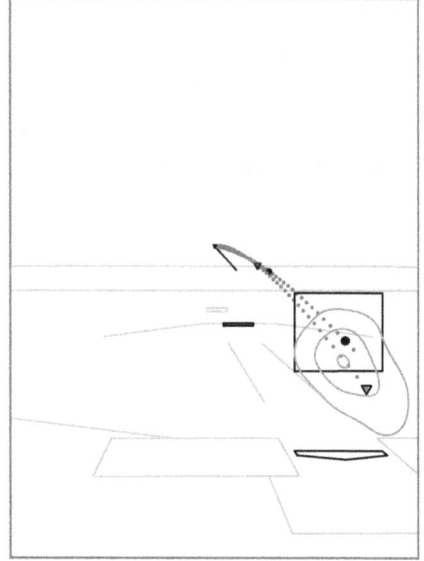

Type	Frequency	Velocity	H Movement	V Movement
● Fastball	37.2%	94.9 [107]	-6.7 [100]	-16.3 [97]
☐ Sinker	5.6%	94.4 [110]	-14.5 [90]	-20.2 [101]
▲ Changeup	12.3%	87.9 [111]	-12.4 [96]	-26.4 [103]
▽ Slider	44.8%	84.4 [102]	4.4 [97]	-34.7 [97]

Colorado Rockies 2021

Daniel Bard RHP
Born: 06/25/85 Age: 36 Bats: R Throws: R
Height: 6'4" Weight: 197 Origin: Round 1, 2006 Draft (#28 overall)

YEAR	TEAM	LVL	AGE	W	L	SV	G	GS	IP	H	HR	BB/9	K/9	K	GB%	BABIP
2020	COL	MLB	35	4	2	6	23	0	24^2	22	2	3.6	9.9	27	48.5%	.312
2021 FS	COL	MLB	36	2	3	21	57	0	50	49	7	5.6	8.1	45	47.9%	.298
2021 DC	COL	MLB	36	2	2	21	49	0	52.3	51	7	5.6	8.1	47	47.9%	.298

Comparables: Pedro Strop, Tyler Clippard, Joe Smith

It was a crisp Boston spring evening. Bard was facing the Houston Astros of the National League. PITCHf/x was all the rage, and Statcast was but a glimmer in its eye. The Boston Marathon bombing had happened a couple weeks prior. "Blurred Lines" just hit the airwaves. Bard looked in and threw ball four to Carlos Corporán. Nine pitches, eight balls. It was April 28, 2013, his last major league appearance and one day before Nolan Arenado's first.

Fast forward seven years, through multiple last-ditch, angst-ridden minor league comebacks, past three years completely free from the merciless grip of organized baseball. Bard entered a dirty inning in a stadium that didn't even have surveyor's marks back then. Now teammates with Arenado, he made four outs without allowing a run (or a walk). In fact, his walk rate, strikeout rate, velocity—all of it—returned to dominance, and all that was required to overcome what the elders call the "yips" was waiting long enough to forget they happened.

Now that we have the technology, we also know he spins fastballs with the fourth-highest rpm in the majors. He even closed out games, more than doubling his career save total. Suddenly it's 2021 and you're glad Daniel Bard is your closer, but can't shake the feeling that Jonathan Papelbon still has the next inning.

YEAR	TEAM	LVL	AGE	WHIP	ERA	DRA-	WARP	MPH	FB%	WHF	CSP
2020	COL	MLB	35	1.30	3.65	79	0.5	98.8	56.3%	28.7%	
2021 FS	COL	MLB	36	1.61	5.62	117	-0.2	98.8	56.3%	28.7%	52.6%
2021 DC	COL	MLB	36	1.61	5.62	117	-0.2	98.8	56.3%	28.7%	52.6%

Daniel Bard, continued

Pitch Shape vs LHH

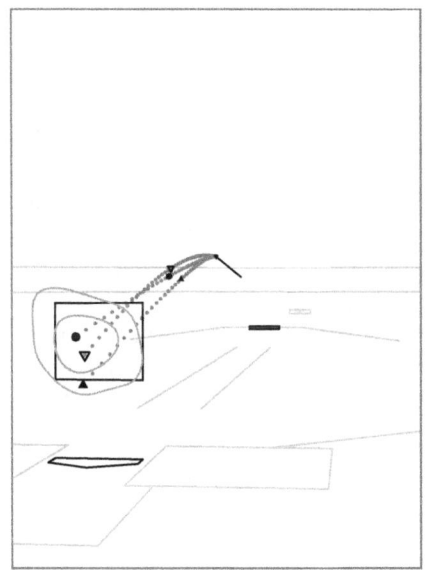

Pitch Shape vs RHH

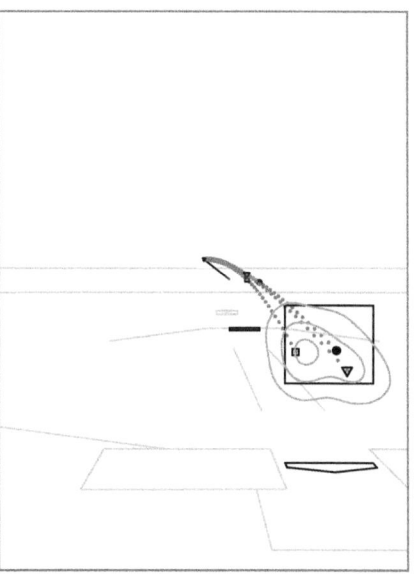

Type	Frequency	Velocity	H Movement	V Movement
● Fastball	42.7%	97.3 [115]	-7.5 [96]	-15.3 [100]
□ Sinker	12.4%	96.6 [121]	-13.3 [98]	-21.3 [98]
▲ Changeup	12.4%	89.8 [118]	-14.5 [85]	-31.6 [89]
▽ Slider	30.3%	87.7 [117]	5.5 [101]	-30.3 [110]

Ryan Castellani RHP

Born: 04/01/96   Age: 25   Bats: R   Throws: R
Height: 6'4"   Weight: 218   Origin: Round 2, 2014 Draft (#48 overall)

YEAR	TEAM	LVL	AGE	W	L	SV	G	GS	IP	H	HR	BB/9	K/9	K	GB%	BABIP
2018	HFD	AA	22	7	9	0	26	26	134[1]	135	15	4.7	6.1	91	37.4%	.293
2019	ABQ	AAA	23	2	5	0	10	10	43[1]	54	14	6.2	9.8	47	44.8%	.336
2020	COL	MLB	24	1	4	0	10	9	43[1]	37	12	5.4	5.2	25	37.6%	.207
2021 FS	COL	MLB	25	8	10	0	26	26	150	157	28	5.0	6.9	114	38.8%	.289
2021 DC	COL	MLB	25	5	7	0	22	21	101	106	19	5.0	6.9	77	38.8%	.289

Comparables: Ariel Jurado, Sean Reid-Foley, Duane Underwood Jr.

Rookie seasons can be unforgiving, but Castellani—thrust into starts out of necessity rather than on merit—had one for the confessional. Returning from a positive COVID-19 test in June, he averaged more than one home run per appearance, threw ball four more often than strike three, had a FIP above 7, and did it all with a BABIP right around .200. Other than that last one, nary a metric cast him in a positive light, and while he was even worse in the PCL the year before that, starting there may be the divine path to statistical forgiveness.

YEAR	TEAM	LVL	AGE	WHIP	ERA	DRA-	WARP	MPH	FB%	WHF	CSP
2018	HFD	AA	22	1.53	5.49	113	0.0				
2019	ABQ	AAA	23	1.94	8.31	164	-0.5				
2020	COL	MLB	24	1.45	5.82	179	-1.4	94.8	49.4%	25.0%	
2021 FS	COL	MLB	25	1.60	5.98	124	-0.6	94.8	49.4%	25.0%	43.8%
2021 DC	COL	MLB	25	1.60	5.98	124	-0.4	94.8	49.4%	25.0%	43.8%

Ryan Castellani, continued

Pitch Shape vs LHH

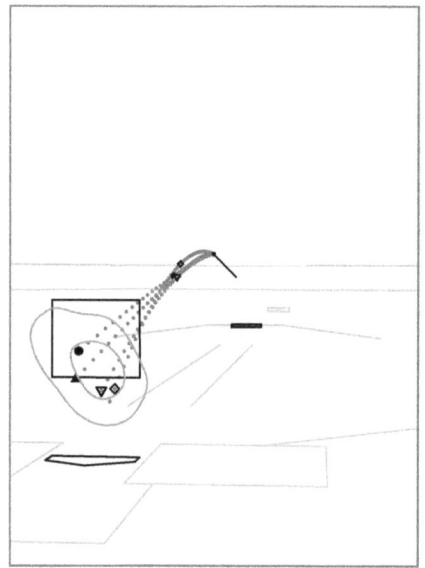

Pitch Shape vs RHH

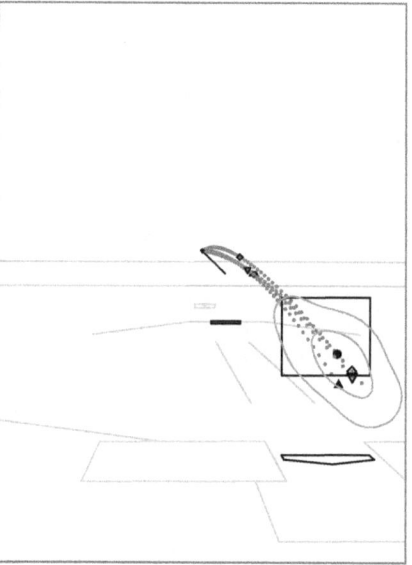

Type	Frequency	Velocity	H Movement	V Movement
● Fastball	44.3%	92.4 [100]	-9.2 [88]	-17.4 [94]
□ Sinker	5.2%	92.5 [101]	-11.4 [112]	-17 [112]
▲ Changeup	16.0%	85.8 [102]	-11.4 [101]	-27.4 [100]
▽ Slider	17.3%	85.1 [105]	2.8 [91]	-31.3 [107]
◇ Curveball	17.3%	79.5 [103]	8.6 [104]	-46.1 [105]

Colorado Rockies 2021

Jairo Díaz   RHP
Born: 05/27/91   Age: 30   Bats: R   Throws: R
Height: 6'0"   Weight: 254   Origin: International Free Agent, 2007

YEAR	TEAM	LVL	AGE	W	L	SV	G	GS	IP	H	HR	BB/9	K/9	K	GB%	BABIP
2019	ABQ	AAA	28	1	0	6	16	0	20	12	0	2.7	9.9	22	64.6%	.250
2019	COL	MLB	28	6	4	5	56	0	57²	56	7	3.0	9.8	63	49.1%	.318
2020	COL	MLB	29	1	2	4	24	0	20	31	4	6.3	7.7	17	40.3%	.409
2021 FS	COL	MLB	30	2	2	0	57	0	50	49	6	4.1	8.5	47	48.2%	.302
2021 DC	COL	MLB	30	2	2	0	43	0	46.3	45	6	4.1	8.5	44	48.2%	.302

Comparables: Hansel Robles, Shawn Armstrong, Mike Morin

Relievers shouldn't aspire to be starters. They should aspire to be commissioners. If Díaz were to run the league, the first thing he'd (presumably) do is allow each reliever to wipe one bad appearance off their stats, because it usually messes up their ERA. In fact, take away one two-out, seven-run nightmare and his 2020 ERA sheds three runs. He would naturally become corrupted with this absolute power, as Lord Acton would suggest. It would turn into scrubbing the stats for all games against one team; suddenly he's removed all the Giants games, now it's down to 3.44. Not satisfied, it would turn into nullifying the numbers for any appearance in which it was raining, or it looked like it was going to rain, or when it was raining somewhere. Suddenly he's accidentally deleted his entire statistical year, we're devoid of data, and we'd say his 2019 looked pretty great, I wonder what he was up to last season, can't wait to see him this year.

YEAR	TEAM	LVL	AGE	WHIP	ERA	DRA-	WARP	MPH	FB%	WHF	CSP
2019	ABQ	AAA	28	0.90	0.45	31	0.9				
2019	COL	MLB	28	1.30	4.53	71	1.2	98.8	56.0%	29.5%	
2020	COL	MLB	29	2.25	7.65	131	-0.2	97.1	57.7%	23.5%	
2021 FS	COL	MLB	30	1.43	4.67	103	0.2	98.2	56.7%	27.2%	46.0%
2021 DC	COL	MLB	30	1.43	4.67	103	0.1	98.2	56.7%	27.2%	46.0%

Jairo Díaz, continued

Pitch Shape vs LHH

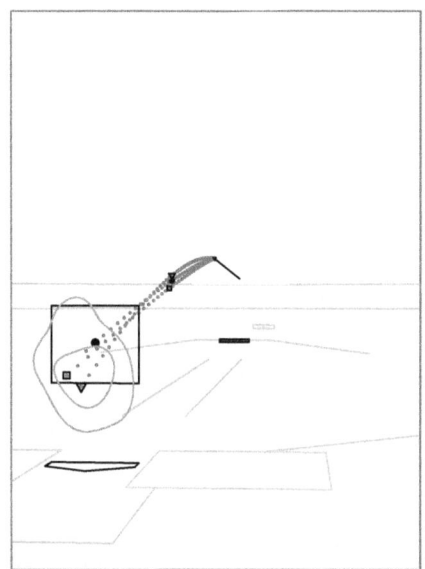

Pitch Shape vs RHH

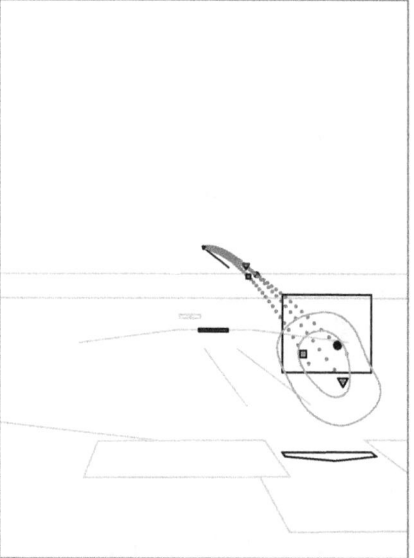

Type	Frequency	Velocity	H Movement	V Movement
● Fastball	23.1%	95.3 [109]	-3.8 [114]	-15.1 [100]
□ Sinker	34.0%	95.1 [114]	-11.7 [110]	-17.7 [109]
▽ Slider	41.8%	85.4 [106]	1.4 [86]	-35.6 [95]

Colorado Rockies 2021

Carlos Estévez RHP
Born: 12/28/92 Age: 28 Bats: R Throws: R
Height: 6'6" Weight: 277 Origin: International Free Agent, 2011

YEAR	TEAM	LVL	AGE	W	L	SV	G	GS	IP	H	HR	BB/9	K/9	K	GB%	BABIP
2018	ABQ	AAA	25	0	1	1	28	0	28^1	37	6	3.5	11.1	35	38.1%	.397
2019	COL	MLB	26	2	2	0	71	0	72	70	12	2.9	10.1	81	38.4%	.305
2020	COL	MLB	27	1	3	1	26	0	24	33	6	3.4	10.1	27	29.9%	.380
2021 FS	COL	MLB	28	2	2	0	57	0	50	45	8	3.4	9.4	52	36.8%	.287
2021 DC	COL	MLB	28	2	2	0	43	0	46.3	42	7	3.4	9.4	48	36.8%	.287

Comparables: Michael Tonkin, Phil Maton, Nick Goody

Having Charlie Sheen's birth name has to grate on a relief pitcher with a big fastball. The two Estévezes have previously met in person but clearly the real pitcher didn't heed the fictional pitcher's cautionary tale of avoiding substandard sequels to breakout performances. He struggled with command throughout the season, becoming a historical footnote when Albert Pujols tied Willie Mays on the home run list thanks to one of his throws. (It is unknown what milestones Clu Haywood touched thanks to The Wild Thing, but we will canonically assume it was several.) The third installment of *Major League* was titled "Back To The Minors." No reason we're mentioning this. Just thought it was neat information.

YEAR	TEAM	LVL	AGE	WHIP	ERA	DRA-	WARP	MPH	FB%	WHF	CSP
2018	ABQ	AAA	25	1.69	6.35	73	0.5				
2019	COL	MLB	26	1.29	3.75	84	1.0	99.7	69.3%	30.7%	
2020	COL	MLB	27	1.75	7.50	123	-0.1	98.7	61.5%	25.1%	
2021 FS	COL	MLB	28	1.28	4.13	93	0.4	99.3	66.6%	28.8%	51.4%
2021 DC	COL	MLB	28	1.28	4.13	93	0.4	99.3	66.6%	28.8%	51.4%

Carlos Estévez, continued

Pitch Shape vs LHH

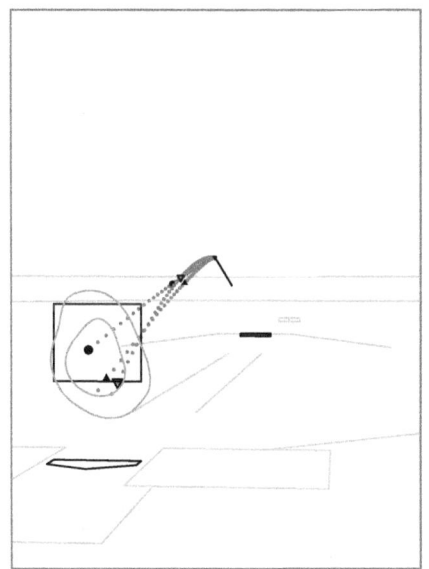

Pitch Shape vs RHH

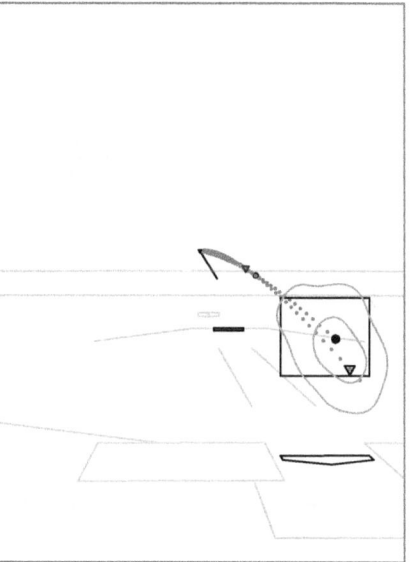

Type	Frequency	Velocity	H Movement	V Movement
● Fastball	61.5%	97 [114]	-7.7 [95]	-12.4 [108]
▲ Changeup	12.4%	88.7 [114]	-10.8 [105]	-25.5 [106]
▽ Slider	26.1%	87 [114]	4.6 [97]	-32.2 [105]

Colorado Rockies 2021

Kyle Freeland   LHP

Born: 05/14/93   Age: 28   Bats: L   Throws: L
Height: 6'4"   Weight: 204   Origin: Round 1, 2014 Draft (#8 overall)

YEAR	TEAM	LVL	AGE	W	L	SV	G	GS	IP	H	HR	BB/9	K/9	K	GB%	BABIP
2018	COL	MLB	25	17	7	0	33	33	202^1	182	17	3.1	7.7	173	45.5%	.288
2019	ABQ	AAA	26	0	4	0	6	6	29^2	40	4	4.9	8.5	28	53.5%	.396
2019	COL	MLB	26	3	11	0	22	22	104^1	126	25	3.4	6.8	79	46.2%	.310
2020	COL	MLB	27	2	3	0	13	13	70^2	77	9	2.9	5.9	46	50.0%	.305
2021 FS	COL	MLB	28	9	8	0	26	26	150	154	21	3.4	7.0	117	49.8%	.297
2021 DC	COL	MLB	28	9	8	0	27	25	147.7	152	20	3.4	7.0	115	49.8%	.297

Comparables: Jordan Montgomery, Daniel Mengden, Cody Reed

   Philosophical question: If you throw a changeup more often than a fastball, is the fastball really the changeup? Freeland blew everyone's augmented minds (it's legal in Colorado, after all) by leaning on the slower option way more than the faster one, especially when behind in the count. The four-seam usage was cut nearly in half, perhaps an adjustment due to a forgettable 2019. Beyond a decent slider he doesn't often get the swing and miss, so his game is getting people off balance and having them stay on the ground. (Because, again, it's legal there.) An admirable philosophy in a stadium built for pitcher nihilism.

YEAR	TEAM	LVL	AGE	WHIP	ERA	DRA-	WARP	MPH	FB%	WHF	CSP
2018	COL	MLB	25	1.25	2.85	86	3.3	93.8	52.5%	21.9%	
2019	ABQ	AAA	26	1.89	8.80	132	0.1				
2019	COL	MLB	26	1.58	6.73	129	-0.6	94.0	52.1%	21.4%	
2020	COL	MLB	27	1.42	4.33	109	0.3	93.9	33.3%	20.6%	
2021 FS	COL	MLB	28	1.40	4.54	101	1.4	93.9	46.0%	21.3%	46.9%
2021 DC	COL	MLB	28	1.40	4.54	101	1.3	93.9	46.0%	21.3%	46.9%

Kyle Freeland, continued

Pitch Shape vs LHH	Pitch Shape vs RHH
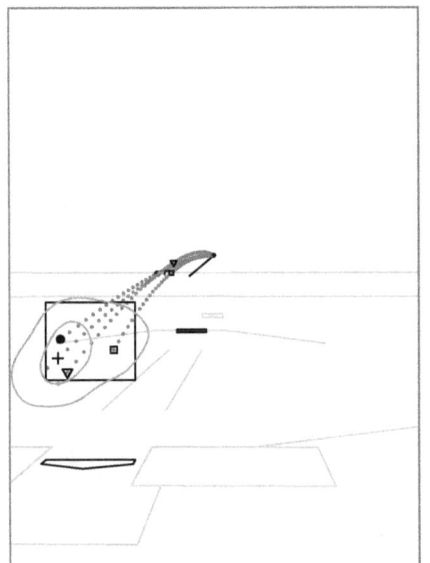	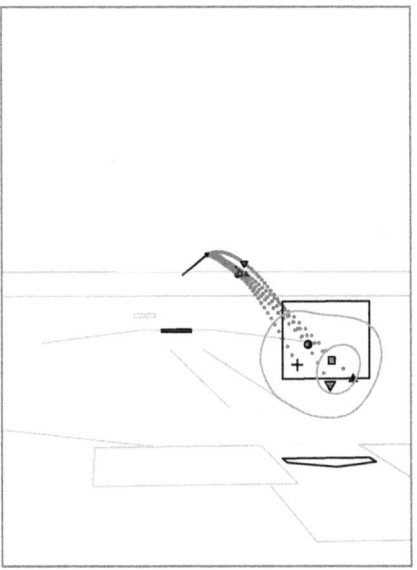

Type	Frequency	Velocity	H Movement	V Movement
● Fastball	21.3%	92.3 [99]	6.4 [102]	-16 [98]
☐ Sinker	12.0%	91.2 [94]	13.1 [100]	-23.4 [91]
+ Cutter	23.7%	86.2 [87]	-1.8 [99]	-28.4 [83]
▲ Changeup	24.1%	86.1 [104]	9.8 [110]	-28.4 [98]
▽ Slider	18.9%	80.3 [84]	-3.7 [94]	-44.1 [70]

Colorado Rockies 2021

Mychal Givens   RHP
Born: 05/13/90   Age: 31   Bats: R   Throws: R
Height: 6'0"   Weight: 230   Origin: Round 2, 2009 Draft (#54 overall)

YEAR	TEAM	LVL	AGE	W	L	SV	G	GS	IP	H	HR	BB/9	K/9	K	GB%	BABIP
2018	BAL	MLB	28	0	7	9	69	0	76^2	61	4	3.5	9.3	79	37.6%	.285
2019	BAL	MLB	29	2	6	11	58	0	63	49	13	3.7	12.3	86	38.4%	.271
2020	COL	MLB	30	1	1	1	22	0	22^1	16	5	4.0	10.1	25	23.2%	.216
2021 FS	COL	MLB	31	2	2	3	57	0	50	41	7	3.8	10.7	59	34.6%	.285
2021 DC	COL	MLB	31	2	2	3	49	0	52.3	43	7	3.8	10.7	62	34.6%	.285

Comparables: Vinnie Pestano, Antonio Bastardo, Jeurys Familia

There are no givens in life, especially when it comes to Rockies pitching, so Jeff Bridich decided to be cute and literally change that by acquiring the longtime Orioles setup man for some infield futures. Prior to the trade, the sidearm slinger began the season with 10 consecutive scoreless innings, thanks to Givens' successful gambit of having batters weakly deposit his pitches into the crab-infused atmosphere on the eastern seaboard. So you don't need much of an imagination to know how that played in the mountains.

YEAR	TEAM	LVL	AGE	WHIP	ERA	DRA-	WARP	MPH	FB%	WHF	CSP
2018	BAL	MLB	28	1.19	3.99	108	0.1	97.4	76.9%	25.0%	
2019	BAL	MLB	29	1.19	4.57	63	1.6	97.5	70.3%	34.2%	
2020	COL	MLB	30	1.16	3.63	113	0.0	96.9	65.1%	27.7%	
2021 FS	COL	MLB	31	1.25	3.69	84	0.7	97.3	70.7%	30.0%	50.6%
2021 DC	COL	MLB	31	1.25	3.69	84	0.7	97.3	70.7%	30.0%	50.6%

Mychal Givens, continued

Pitch Shape vs LHH

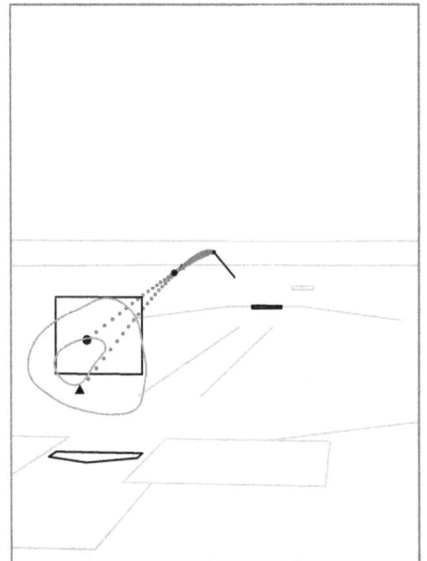

Pitch Shape vs RHH

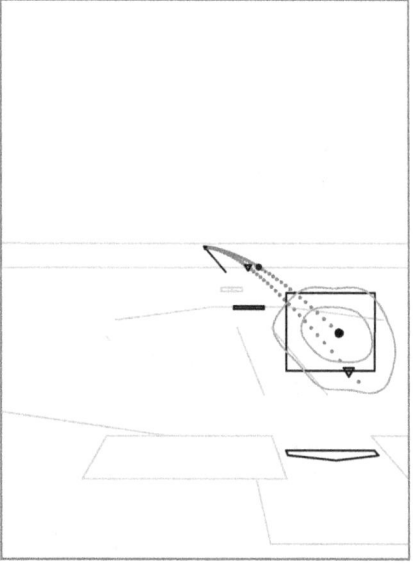

Type	Frequency	Velocity	H Movement	V Movement
● Fastball	64.8%	94.7 [107]	-8.4 [92]	-16 [98]
▲ Changeup	18.8%	82.9 [91]	-10.3 [108]	-38.7 [69]
▽ Slider	16.1%	85 [105]	3.5 [93]	-29.5 [112]

Colorado Rockies 2021

Austin Gomber LHP
Born: 11/23/93 Age: 27 Bats: L Throws: L
Height: 6'5" Weight: 220 Origin: Round 4, 2014 Draft (#135 overall)

YEAR	TEAM	LVL	AGE	W	L	SV	G	GS	IP	H	HR	BB/9	K/9	K	GB%	BABIP
2018	MEM	AAA	24	7	3	0	12	11	68^1	65	9	2.6	10.0	76	38.1%	.315
2018	STL	MLB	24	6	2	0	30	12	81^1	83	8	3.8	8.1	73	38.1%	.322
2019	MEM	AAA	25	4	0	0	8	8	45^1	42	5	3.2	10.3	52	37.6%	.333
2020	STL	MLB	26	1	1	0	14	4	29	19	1	4.7	8.4	27	48.0%	.243
2021 FS	COL	MLB	27	9	8	0	26	26	150	138	21	3.9	9.1	152	42.5%	.294
2021 DC	COL	MLB	27	6	5	0	48	8	71.3	66	10	3.9	9.1	72	42.5%	.294

Comparables: Jalen Beeks, Rookie Davis, Eric Skoglund

Gomber bounced back from an injury-plagued 2019 to post a breakthrough season in a swingman role. He's a tall drink of water who lives in the low-90s with his fastball and who relies on his knuckle-curve (along with an improving slider and the occasional changeup) to keep batters off-balance and induce weak contact. Gomber uncharacteristically struggled a bit with his control last year but that shouldn't be a long-term concern. He's not likely to post another sub-2 ERA and there's nothing exciting about his profile, but Gomber has shown the steady competence necessary to survive at the back end of the rotation or in long relief.

YEAR	TEAM	LVL	AGE	WHIP	ERA	DRA-	WARP	MPH	FB%	WHF	CSP
2018	MEM	AAA	24	1.24	3.42	58	2.2				
2018	STL	MLB	24	1.44	4.32	110	0.2	95.0	50.4%	21.9%	
2019	MEM	AAA	25	1.28	2.98	57	1.7				
2020	STL	MLB	26	1.17	1.86	95	0.3	94.0	52.5%	26.6%	
2021 FS	COL	MLB	27	1.36	4.24	94	1.9	94.4	51.6%	24.5%	49.2%
2021 DC	COL	MLB	27	1.36	4.24	94	0.8	94.4	51.6%	24.5%	49.2%

Austin Gomber, continued

Pitch Shape vs LHH

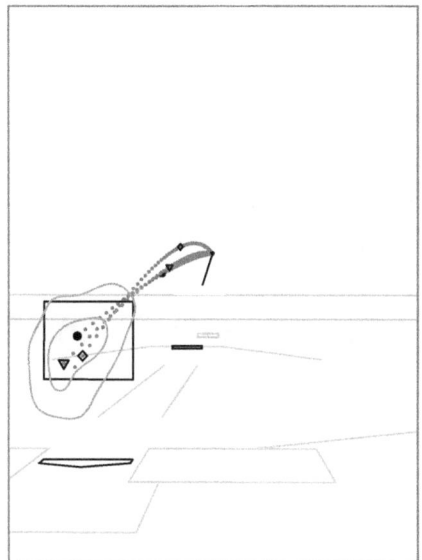

Pitch Shape vs RHH

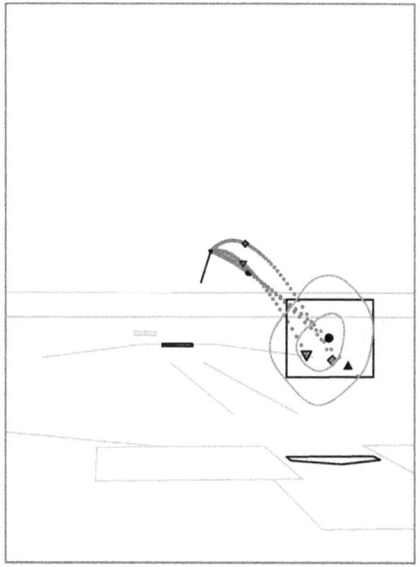

Type	Frequency	Velocity	H Movement	V Movement
● Fastball	52.5%	92.7 [100]	4.9 [109]	-12 [109]
▲ Changeup	7.4%	83.4 [93]	9.3 [113]	-24.6 [108]
▽ Slider	15.8%	86.1 [110]	-4.7 [98]	-30.4 [110]
◇ Curveball	24.3%	76.6 [92]	-5.1 [90]	-57.2 [80]

Colorado Rockies 2021

Chi Chi González RHP
Born: 01/15/92 Age: 29 Bats: R Throws: R
Height: 6'3" Weight: 210 Origin: Round 1, 2013 Draft (#23 overall)

YEAR	TEAM	LVL	AGE	W	L	SV	G	GS	IP	H	HR	BB/9	K/9	K	GB%	BABIP
2019	ABQ	AAA	27	4	5	0	16	15	87	105	15	3.7	7.9	76	50.4%	.345
2019	COL	MLB	27	2	6	0	14	12	63	59	11	4.7	6.6	46	42.9%	.261
2020	COL	MLB	28	0	2	0	6	4	19^2	22	3	4.6	7.3	16	35.5%	.328
2021 FS	COL	MLB	29	2	3	0	57	0	50	51	8	4.0	7.2	40	44.1%	.296

Comparables: P.J. Walters, José Ureña, Tyler Chatwood

The best thing that can be said about González's season is he swapped out his slider for a curveball. Perhaps the second-best thing that can be said for someone whose offerings were bludgeoned about the ballpark was that at least there weren't more home runs.

YEAR	TEAM	LVL	AGE	WHIP	ERA	DRA-	WARP	MPH	FB%	WHF	CSP
2019	ABQ	AAA	27	1.62	6.10	99	1.6				
2019	COL	MLB	27	1.46	5.29	126	-0.3	94.0	54.8%	20.5%	
2020	COL	MLB	28	1.63	6.86	119	0.0	94.2	59.9%	18.7%	
2021 FS	COL	MLB	29	1.49	5.19	112	-0.1	94.1	56.4%	19.9%	46.3%

Chi Chi González, continued

Pitch Shape vs LHH

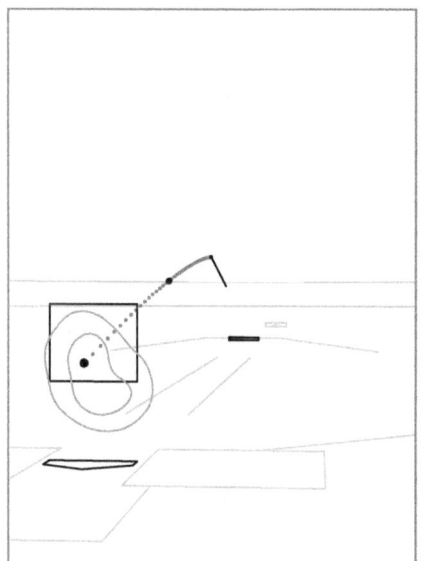

Pitch Shape vs RHH

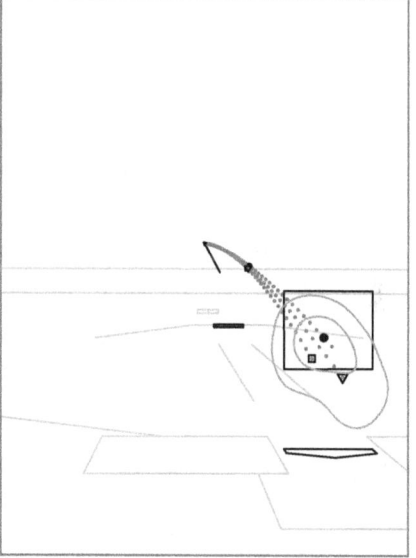

Type	Frequency	Velocity	H Movement	V Movement
● Fastball	45.0%	92.3 [99]	-1.9 [123]	-18.5 [91]
☐ Sinker	15.0%	92 [98]	-9.1 [129]	-21.6 [96]
▲ Changeup	13.0%	86.9 [107]	-10.7 [105]	-29.4 [95]
▽ Slider	19.6%	87 [114]	1.7 [87]	-28.1 [116]
◇ Curveball	7.5%	81.1 [110]	3.8 [85]	-37.8 [124]

Colorado Rockies 2021

Jon Gray RHP

Born: 11/05/91   Age: 29   Bats: R   Throws: R
Height: 6'4"   Weight: 225   Origin: Round 1, 2013 Draft (#3 overall)

YEAR	TEAM	LVL	AGE	W	L	SV	G	GS	IP	H	HR	BB/9	K/9	K	GB%	BABIP
2018	ABQ	AAA	26	1	0	0	2	2	10^2	7	1	3.4	11.0	13	63.0%	.231
2018	COL	MLB	26	12	9	0	31	31	172^1	180	27	2.7	9.6	183	47.5%	.326
2019	COL	MLB	27	11	8	0	26	25	150	147	19	3.4	8.9	149	49.9%	.318
2020	COL	MLB	28	2	4	0	8	8	39	45	6	2.5	5.1	22	36.7%	.293
2021 FS	COL	MLB	29	9	8	0	26	26	150	150	23	3.2	7.9	131	43.4%	.297
2021 DC	COL	MLB	29	9	8	0	25	25	142.3	142	22	3.2	7.9	125	43.4%	.297

Comparables: Kevin Gausman, Vince Velasquez, Jake Odorizzi

It's a love story you've heard many times: Boy finds baseball. Boy loves baseball. Boy throws baseball hard. Boy finds major league team. Major league team is the Rockies. Boy's ERA swells up to the size of a genetically-modified grapefruit. By "love story" it would have been more appropriate to say "horror story," and Elisabeth Kübler-Ross did once say there are only two real human emotions, love and fear. So there is nothing more human than spending six seasons as a Rockies pitcher, and Gray is one of the few who has truly lived.

YEAR	TEAM	LVL	AGE	WHIP	ERA	DRA-	WARP	MPH	FB%	WHF	CSP
2018	ABQ	AAA	26	1.03	3.38	70	0.3				
2018	COL	MLB	26	1.35	5.12	99	1.7	96.9	49.7%	29.2%	
2019	COL	MLB	27	1.35	3.84	81	2.9	97.8	52.7%	26.3%	
2020	COL	MLB	28	1.44	6.69	136	-0.4	95.4	49.4%	22.1%	
2021 FS	COL	MLB	29	1.36	4.47	99	1.5	97.0	51.1%	26.3%	48.3%
2021 DC	COL	MLB	29	1.36	4.47	99	1.4	97.0	51.1%	26.3%	48.3%

Jon Gray, continued

Pitch Shape vs LHH	Pitch Shape vs RHH
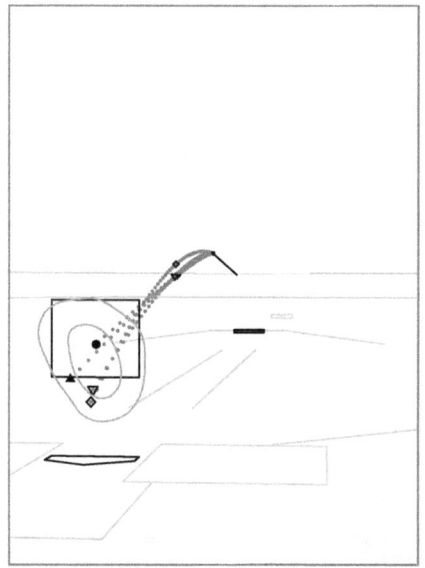	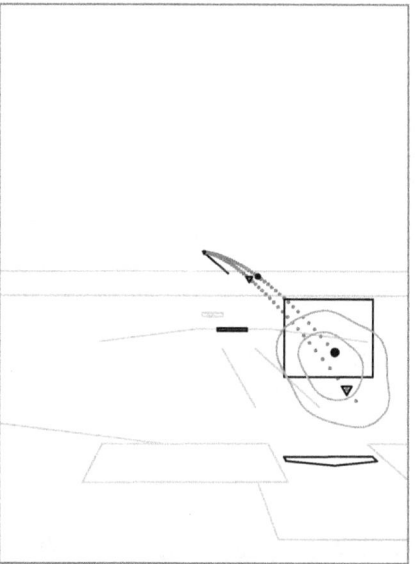

Type	Frequency	Velocity	H Movement	V Movement
● Fastball	49.1%	94.1 [105]	-10.1 [84]	-17.4 [94]
▲ Changeup	13.1%	86.5 [105]	-9.1 [114]	-22.1 [115]
▽ Slider	29.2%	86.4 [111]	2.5 [90]	-28.7 [115]
◇ Curveball	8.4%	77.8 [97]	8.7 [104]	-45 [108]

Colorado Rockies 2021

Tyler Kinley   RHP

Born: 01/31/91   Age: 30   Bats: R   Throws: R
Height: 6'4"   Weight: 220   Origin: Round 16, 2013 Draft (#472 overall)

YEAR	TEAM	LVL	AGE	W	L	SV	G	GS	IP	H	HR	BB/9	K/9	K	GB%	BABIP
2018	NO	AAA	27	2	2	8	40	0	40	32	2	5.0	12.6	56	38.3%	.326
2018	MIA	MLB	27	0	0	0	9	0	7^2	6	0	4.7	10.6	9	55.0%	.300
2018	MIN	MLB	27	0	0	0	4	0	3^1	9	2	10.8	10.8	4	60.0%	.538
2019	NO	AAA	28	0	1	2	14	0	15^2	4	1	4.0	10.9	19	35.5%	.100
2019	MIA	MLB	28	3	1	1	52	0	49^1	43	5	6.6	8.4	46	38.4%	.288
2020	COL	MLB	29	0	2	0	24	0	23^2	13	2	4.6	9.9	26	45.5%	.212
2021 FS	COL	MLB	30	2	2	0	57	0	50	43	7	5.2	10.3	57	41.3%	.296
2021 DC	COL	MLB	30	2	2	0	49	0	52.3	46	7	5.2	10.3	59	41.3%	.296

Comparables: Emilio Pagán, Jacob Barnes, Ryan Dull

Kinley is a one-card reliever, but it's a dominant-suit face card: "try and hit my slider." It's one of the league's best, but as is the case with singular sensations, this has led to a chorus line of walks. The fastball is serviceable, but even for sitting at 96 mph, it's surprisingly hittable. Kinley's job when he gets into the game is making everybody looking on—batter, catcher, umpire, fielders, manager, himself—a little more uncomfortable than normal, which is the entire point of baseball, admittedly.

YEAR	TEAM	LVL	AGE	WHIP	ERA	DRA-	WARP	MPH	FB%	WHF	CSP
2018	NO	AAA	27	1.35	2.92	50	1.3				
2018	MIA	MLB	27	1.30	7.04	51	0.2	98.7	55.4%	29.4%	
2018	MIN	MLB	27	3.90	24.30	58	0.1	97.5	67.9%	33.3%	
2019	NO	AAA	28	0.70	1.72	36	0.7				
2019	MIA	MLB	28	1.60	3.65	119	-0.3	96.3	42.3%	29.5%	
2020	COL	MLB	29	1.06	5.32	86	0.4	97.3	33.6%	36.2%	
2021 FS	COL	MLB	30	1.46	4.56	98	0.3	96.8	40.3%	32.1%	43.0%
2021 DC	COL	MLB	30	1.46	4.56	98	0.3	96.8	40.3%	32.1%	43.0%

Tyler Kinley, continued

Pitch Shape vs LHH

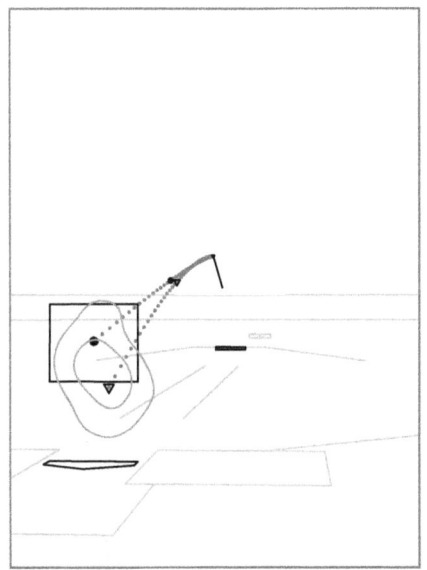

Pitch Shape vs RHH

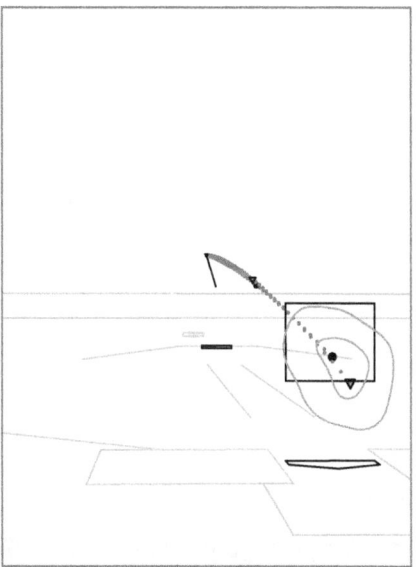

Type	Frequency	Velocity	H Movement	V Movement
● Fastball	33.1%	96 [111]	-3.7 [114]	-12.1 [109]
▲ Changeup	6.7%	88.3 [112]	-10 [109]	-21.5 [116]
▽ Slider	59.7%	89.5 [125]	2.7 [90]	-27.2 [119]

Germán Márquez   RHP

Born: 02/22/95   Age: 26   Bats: R   Throws: R
Height: 6'1"   Weight: 230   Origin: International Free Agent, 2011

YEAR	TEAM	LVL	AGE	W	L	SV	G	GS	IP	H	HR	BB/9	K/9	K	GB%	BABIP
2018	COL	MLB	23	14	11	0	33	33	196	179	24	2.6	10.6	230	47.3%	.314
2019	COL	MLB	24	12	5	0	28	28	174	174	29	1.8	9.1	175	48.2%	.308
2020	COL	MLB	25	4	6	0	13	13	81²	78	6	2.8	8.0	73	50.4%	.300
2021 FS	COL	MLB	26	10	7	0	26	26	150	142	20	2.6	8.8	146	48.8%	.298
2021 DC	COL	MLB	26	11	8	0	27	27	170.7	161	23	2.6	8.8	166	48.8%	.298

Comparables: Luis Severino, Lucas Giolito, José Berríos

We've spent several paragraphs over the years discussing the merits of Márquez's ace status using the advanced numbers. If you're sick of the long division, then let's stare at the raw ones for a second: In each of his starts, he always made it five innings and once made it into the eighth. He allowed at least one run in each of his starts. He was second in the league in innings and tied for the lead in batters faced. Liván Hernández may weep at the state of innings eaters these days, but Márquez is the modern day gourmand. Now back to the calculus: While his DRA isn't even in the top 50, his workload multiplies that into a top 20 pitcher, or a second-tier ace. You may not like it, but this is what peak performance looks like.

YEAR	TEAM	LVL	AGE	WHIP	ERA	DRA-	WARP	MPH	FB%	WHF	CSP
2018	COL	MLB	23	1.20	3.77	72	4.7	97.5	55.0%	28.4%	
2019	COL	MLB	24	1.20	4.76	66	4.7	97.7	52.1%	26.8%	
2020	COL	MLB	25	1.26	3.75	79	1.7	97.9	52.4%	26.3%	
2021 FS	COL	MLB	26	1.24	3.76	86	2.6	97.7	52.9%	27.1%	50.1%
2021 DC	COL	MLB	26	1.24	3.76	86	2.9	97.7	52.9%	27.1%	50.1%

Germán Márquez, continued

Pitch Shape vs LHH

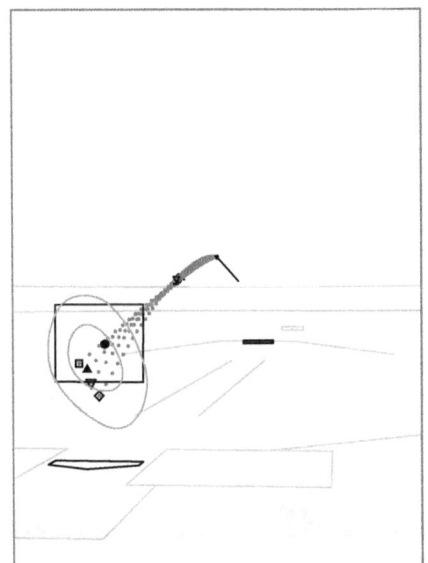

Pitch Shape vs RHH

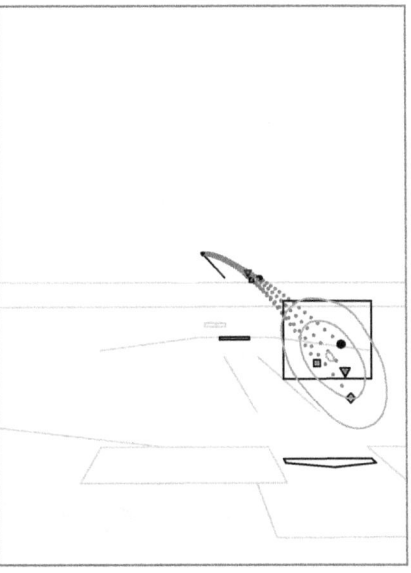

Type	Frequency	Velocity	H Movement	V Movement
● Fastball	38.2%	96 [111]	-6.1 [103]	-14.3 [102]
□ Sinker	14.2%	94.8 [112]	-11.8 [110]	-19.1 [105]
▲ Changeup	5.6%	86.9 [107]	-11.7 [100]	-23.9 [110]
▽ Slider	17.5%	88 [118]	0.6 [82]	-27.8 [117]
◇ Curveball	24.6%	85.5 [127]	3.2 [82]	-36.2 [127]

Colorado Rockies 2021

Antonio Senzatela RHP
Born: 01/21/95 Age: 26 Bats: R Throws: R
Height: 6'1" Weight: 236 Origin: International Free Agent, 2011

YEAR	TEAM	LVL	AGE	W	L	SV	G	GS	IP	H	HR	BB/9	K/9	K	GB%	BABIP
2018	ABQ	AAA	23	3	1	0	8	8	37²	29	1	2.9	10.0	42	47.4%	.301
2018	COL	MLB	23	6	6	0	23	13	90¹	94	10	3.0	6.9	69	46.5%	.303
2019	ABQ	AAA	24	1	1	0	7	7	34¹	45	7	2.6	3.1	12	48.4%	.317
2019	COL	MLB	24	11	11	0	25	25	124²	161	19	4.1	5.5	76	53.5%	.336
2020	COL	MLB	25	5	3	0	12	12	73¹	71	9	2.2	5.0	41	50.8%	.268
2021 FS	COL	MLB	26	9	9	0	26	26	150	161	23	3.2	6.0	100	50.0%	.294
2021 DC	COL	MLB	26	8	9	0	27	25	145	156	23	3.2	6.0	97	50.0%	.294

Comparables: Zach Eflin, Erasmo Ramírez, Tyler Mahle

Look, they're all underrated pitchers. They can't all be Kershaws and Scherzers. Bury the u-word when discussing Senzatela, and discuss him often because that name comfortably rolls off the tongue. The Rockies righty finished in the NL's top 10 in home runs per nine and walks per nine. That he accomplished this as a Coorsman with the league's absolute worst strikeout rate meant the fielders, they were busy. Since he can pitch deep into games and avoid the two bad true outcomes with the ground game, he'll be rated just fine.

YEAR	TEAM	LVL	AGE	WHIP	ERA	DRA-	WARP	MPH	FB%	WHF	CSP
2018	ABQ	AAA	23	1.09	2.15	92	0.5				
2018	COL	MLB	23	1.37	4.38	114	0.1	96.0	64.1%	20.9%	
2019	ABQ	AAA	24	1.60	5.77	115	0.4				
2019	COL	MLB	24	1.75	6.71	146	-1.9	95.9	63.7%	17.9%	
2020	COL	MLB	25	1.21	3.44	101	0.6	96.5	56.0%	18.5%	
2021 FS	COL	MLB	26	1.44	4.96	109	0.7	96.1	61.0%	18.6%	48.4%
2021 DC	COL	MLB	26	1.44	4.96	109	0.7	96.1	61.0%	18.6%	48.4%

Antonio Senzatela, continued

Pitch Shape vs LHH

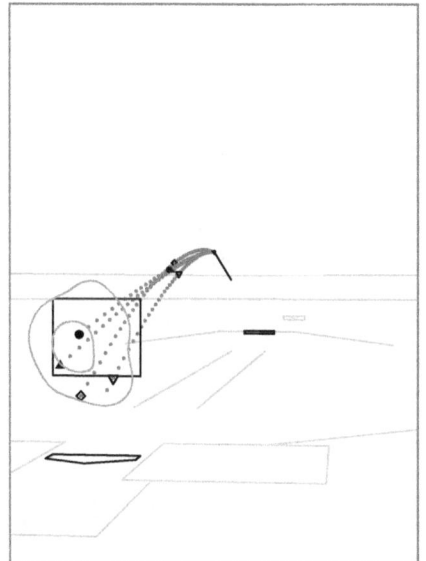

Pitch Shape vs RHH

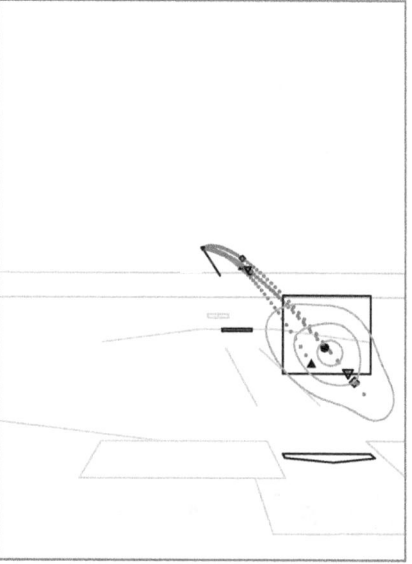

Type	Frequency	Velocity	H Movement	V Movement
● Fastball	56.0%	94.4 [106]	-5.3 [107]	-17.8 [93]
▲ Changeup	10.3%	86.4 [105]	-7.4 [123]	-24.9 [107]
▽ Slider	24.5%	86.5 [111]	4.6 [97]	-30.7 [109]
◇ Curveball	9.2%	79.4 [103]	6.7 [96]	-44.6 [108]

Colorado Rockies 2021

Robert Stephenson RHP
Born: 02/24/93 Age: 28 Bats: R Throws: R
Height: 6'3" Weight: 205 Origin: Round 1, 2011 Draft (#27 overall)

YEAR	TEAM	LVL	AGE	W	L	SV	G	GS	IP	H	HR	BB/9	K/9	K	GB%	BABIP
2018	LOU	AAA	25	11	6	0	20	20	113	74	12	4.5	10.8	135	38.0%	.240
2018	CIN	MLB	25	0	2	0	4	3	11^2	17	2	9.3	8.5	11	32.5%	.395
2019	CIN	MLB	26	3	2	0	57	0	64^2	43	9	3.3	11.3	81	31.4%	.231
2020	CIN	MLB	27	0	0	0	10	0	10	11	8	2.7	11.7	13	23.1%	.167
2021 FS	COL	MLB	28	2	2	0	57	0	50	43	9	4.8	11.0	61	33.6%	.292
2021 DC	COL	MLB	28	2	2	0	43	0	46.3	40	8	4.8	11.0	57	33.6%	.292

Comparables: Jeff Hoffman, Matt Wisler, John Gant

You know how we so often write that a reliever with iffy command and fly-ball tendencies always runs the risk of a sudden, random bout of gopheritis crushing their season? That was Stephenson last year, who followed up his long-anticipated 2019 bullpen breakout by allowing eight home runs in 10 innings, with fully half of the fly balls he allowed landing in the bleachers. He also missed most of August with a sore back, so like all the other disappointing Stephenson years it's best to just let the river wash this one away and move on. The swing-and-miss stuff remains undeniable, but time is no longer on Stephenson's side.

YEAR	TEAM	LVL	AGE	WHIP	ERA	DRA-	WARP	MPH	FB%	WHF	CSP
2018	LOU	AAA	25	1.16	2.87	75	2.3				
2018	CIN	MLB	25	2.49	9.26	145	-0.2	94.7	36.4%	25.5%	
2019	CIN	MLB	26	1.04	3.76	77	1.1	96.6	36.2%	39.0%	
2020	CIN	MLB	27	1.40	9.90	140	-0.1	96.1	30.1%	39.5%	
2021 FS	COL	MLB	28	1.40	4.63	101	0.2	96.3	35.0%	37.9%	44.3%
2021 DC	COL	MLB	28	1.40	4.63	101	0.2	96.3	35.0%	37.9%	44.3%

Robert Stephenson, continued

Pitch Shape vs LHH

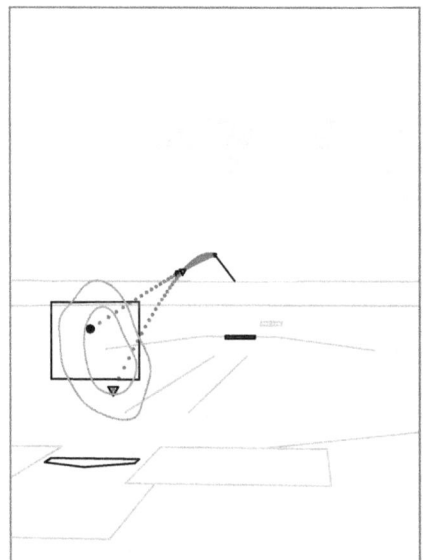

Pitch Shape vs RHH

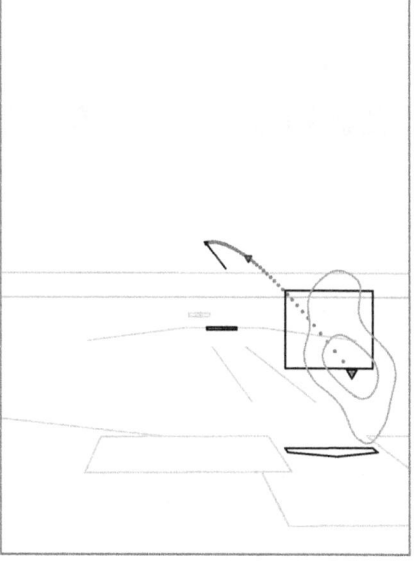

Type	Frequency	Velocity	H Movement	V Movement
● Fastball	29.8%	95 [108]	-11 [79]	-11.8 [110]
▲ Changeup	3.9%	86.8 [106]	-8.8 [115]	-19.4 [122]
▽ Slider	65.2%	83.8 [99]	2.8 [91]	-36.4 [92]

PLAYER COMMENTS WITHOUT GRAPHS

C.J. Cron 1B
Born: 01/05/90 Age: 31 Bats: R Throws: R
Height: 6'4" Weight: 235 Origin: Round 1, 2011 Draft (#17 overall)

YEAR	TEAM	LVL	AGE	PA	R	2B	3B	HR	RBI	BB	K	SB	CS	AVG/OBP/SLG
2018	TB	MLB	28	560	68	28	1	30	74	37	145	1	2	.253/.323/.493
2019	MIN	MLB	29	499	51	24	0	25	78	29	107	0	0	.253/.311/.469
2020	DET	MLB	30	52	9	3	0	4	8	9	16	0	0	.190/.346/.548
2021 FS	COL	MLB	31	600	76	25	2	31	89	40	156	2	2	.247/.317/.477
2021 DC	COL	MLB	31	398	50	17	1	21	59	27	104	2	1	.247/.317/.477

Comparables: Matt Adams, Mark Trumbo, Andres Galarraga

Seven of Cron's eight hits went for extra bases and half cleared the wall. A walking obelisk of ISO, said walking turned into a severe limp that required knee surgery, limiting his 2020 to two weeks of bopping and a pocketful of what-ifs. He was already on a trajectory of nothing but one-year deals for the rest of his career, plugging into lineup sinkholes wherever they may arise, because when you're a right-handed first baseman, it's a little-known rule that you can only sign one-year or 10-year deals.

YEAR	TEAM	LVL	AGE	PA	DRC+	BABIP	BRR	FRAA	WARP
2018	TB	MLB	28	560	117	.293	-3.5	1B(61): 2.6	1.9
2019	MIN	MLB	29	499	100	.277	-2.6	1B(117): 8.0	1.3
2020	DET	MLB	30	52	99	.182	-0.3	1B(13): 1.1	0.2
2021 FS	COL	MLB	31	600	110	.291	-0.4	1B 3	1.9
2021 DC	COL	MLB	31	398	110	.291	-0.3	1B 2	1.3

Yonathan Daza   LF

Born: 02/28/94   Age: 27   Bats: R   Throws: R
Height: 6'2"   Weight: 207   Origin: International Free Agent, 2010

YEAR	TEAM	LVL	AGE	PA	R	2B	3B	HR	RBI	BB	K	SB	CS	AVG/OBP/SLG
2018	HFD	AA	24	228	27	18	2	4	29	7	24	4	5	.306/.330/.461
2019	ABQ	AAA	25	418	67	30	4	11	48	25	52	12	9	.364/.404/.548
2019	COL	MLB	25	105	7	1	1	0	3	7	21	1	0	.206/.257/.237
2021 FS	COL	MLB	27	600	58	25	5	11	59	29	127	5	4	.257/.301/.381
2021 DC	COL	MLB	27	398	38	17	3	7	39	19	84	3	3	.257/.301/.381

Comparables: Xavier Paul, Jason Bourgeois, Charlie Blackmon

Prospect development is not linear; in fact, sometimes, it's a mobius strip. To put it in perspective, Daza's been in the Rockies' system for longer than Airbnb has been in existence. There's no question about his ability to patrol center field, but the other half of the inning only looks good if the suddenly 27-year-old is in the PCL.

YEAR	TEAM	LVL	AGE	PA	DRC+	BABIP	BRR	FRAA	WARP
2018	HFD	AA	24	228	117	.330	-0.6	CF(30): 1.3, RF(16): 4.2, LF(4): -1.0	1.1
2019	ABQ	AAA	25	418	122	.399	-1.2	CF(87): 4.1, LF(2): 0.0	2.8
2019	COL	MLB	25	105	59	.260	1.2	CF(24): -0.5, LF(3): 1.0, RF(3): 0.1	0.0
2021 FS	COL	MLB	27	600	83	.316	0.4	CF 2, RF -1	0.6
2021 DC	COL	MLB	27	398	83	.316	0.3	CF 1, RF 0	0.2

Niko Decolati   RF

Born: 08/12/97   Age: 23   Bats: R   Throws: R
Height: 6'1"   Weight: 215   Origin: Round 6, 2018 Draft (#186 overall)

YEAR	TEAM	LVL	AGE	PA	R	2B	3B	HR	RBI	BB	K	SB	CS	AVG/OBP/SLG
2018	GJ	ROK	20	304	55	15	3	11	56	34	56	17	5	.327/.414/.532
2019	ASH	LO-A	21	331	42	13	4	6	38	13	80	15	6	.265/.334/.399
2021 FS	COL	MLB	23	600	49	22	3	8	51	39	187	12	6	.208/.276/.310

Comparables: Whit Merrifield, Aaron Altherr, Alex Presley

A Boulder native, Decolati is hoping his athleticism will turn him into a major league outfielder, because right now he just sounds like the largest boulder in northern Italy.

YEAR	TEAM	LVL	AGE	PA	DRC+	BABIP	BRR	FRAA	WARP
2018	GJ	ROK	20	304		.381			
2019	ASH	LO-A	21	331	89	.341	0.4	CF(57): -1.7, RF(17): 2.2	0.7
2021 FS	COL	MLB	23	600	64	.300	1.1	RF 6, CF 1	-0.4

Colorado Rockies 2021

Ian Desmond CF
Born: 09/20/85 Age: 35 Bats: R Throws: R
Height: 6'3" Weight: 217 Origin: Round 3, 2004 Draft (#84 overall)

YEAR	TEAM	LVL	AGE	PA	R	2B	3B	HR	RBI	BB	K	SB	CS	AVG/OBP/SLG
2018	COL	MLB	32	619	82	21	8	22	88	53	146	20	6	.236/.307/.422
2019	COL	MLB	33	482	64	31	4	20	65	34	119	3	3	.255/.310/.479
2021 FS	COL	MLB	35	600	65	21	4	18	67	44	174	15	6	.229/.294/.385

Comparables: Jhonny Peralta, Dale Sveum, Chris Woodward

Desmond had a pretty good season in 2020. Sure, by opting out of the year for COVID-19 concerns, he fell 0.1 WARP shy of his PECOTA projections. But the oft-maligned shortstop-turned-first baseman-turned-center fielder made an impassioned post on Instagram, explaining how the Black Lives Matter protest had cemented his own feelings about the issues of race facing baseball. He was particularly concerned about the accessibility issues facing poorer children in the era of expensive travel ball. He spent the summer helping his family, while also working to re-establish the Sarasota Youth Baseball Program where he himself had started down his path. It was a small victory, and it'll create more small victories and start kids walking down their own paths, long after the 2020 season is just a memory.

YEAR	TEAM	LVL	AGE	PA	DRC+	BABIP	BRR	FRAA	WARP
2018	COL	MLB	32	619	89	.279	0.8	1B(138): -2.6, LF(18): 0.8, SS(3): -0.1	0.2
2019	COL	MLB	33	482	85	.304	0.4	CF(74): -12.8, LF(44): -2.9, P(1): -0.0	-0.8
2021 FS	COL	MLB	35	600	82	.302	1.5	1B 1, CF -3	-0.2

Grant Lavigne 1B
Born: 08/27/99 Age: 21 Bats: L Throws: R
Height: 6'4" Weight: 220 Origin: Round 1, 2018 Draft (#42 overall)

YEAR	TEAM	LVL	AGE	PA	R	2B	3B	HR	RBI	BB	K	SB	CS	AVG/OBP/SLG
2018	GJ	ROK	18	258	45	13	2	6	38	45	40	12	7	.350/.477/.519
2019	ASH	LO-A	19	526	52	19	0	7	64	68	129	8	9	.236/.347/.327
2021 FS	COL	MLB	21	600	50	22	2	7	49	48	180	3	3	.212/.285/.305

Comparables: Ronald Guzmán, Eric Hosmer, Dominic Smith

After laying waste to rookie ball in 2018, Lavigne took on the challenge of Low-A in 2019 and fell flat. That, combined with the forced sabbatical of 2020, might cause one to think there are unanswered questions here, but no. It's pretty straightforward: If he hits home runs, he's going to be a good first baseman. If he doesn't, he won't. He's the first Lavigne to not be associated with being complicated.

YEAR	TEAM	LVL	AGE	PA	DRC+	BABIP	BRR	FRAA	WARP
2018	GJ	ROK	18	258		.410			
2019	ASH	LO-A	19	526	87	.314	-4.4	1B(112): 0.9	-0.5
2021 FS	COL	MLB	21	600	65	.303	-0.4	1B -2	-2.1

Elehuris Montero 3B

Born: 08/17/98 Age: 22 Bats: R Throws: R
Height: 6'3" Weight: 235 Origin: International Free Agent, 2014

YEAR	TEAM	LVL	AGE	PA	R	2B	3B	HR	RBI	BB	K	SB	CS	AVG/OBP/SLG
2018	PEO	LO-A	19	425	68	28	3	15	69	33	81	2	0	.322/.381/.529
2018	PMB	HI-A	19	106	13	9	0	1	13	5	22	1	0	.286/.330/.408
2019	SPR	AA	20	238	23	8	0	7	18	14	74	0	1	.188/.235/.317
2021 FS	COL	MLB	22	600	63	22	2	18	62	35	193	0	1	.212/.266/.358
2021 DC	COL	MLB	22	128	13	4	0	3	13	7	41	0	0	.212/.266/.358

Comparables: Josh Vitters, Nick Castellanos, Dilson Herrera

Fate kept Montero from getting another crack at Double-A to prove his punchless 2019 was a mere injury-marred blip; time and plus raw power are in his corner, but contact issues and a lack of athleticism that might force him across the diamond are threatening to knock his prospect status cold.

YEAR	TEAM	LVL	AGE	PA	DRC+	BABIP	BRR	FRAA	WARP
2018	PEO	LO-A	19	425	163	.372	0.3	3B(77): 2.7	4.0
2018	PMB	HI-A	19	106	116	.355	0.6	3B(20): 0.8	0.4
2019	SPR	AA	20	238	33	.245	-0.4	3B(52): -6.2	-1.4
2021 FS	COL	MLB	22	600	66	.291	-0.6	3B -3	-1.9
2021 DC	COL	MLB	22	128	66	.291	-0.1	3B -1	-0.4

Roberto Ramos 1B

Born: 12/28/94   Age: 26   Bats: L   Throws: R
Height: 6'3"   Weight: 220   Origin: Round 16, 2014 Draft (#473 overall)

YEAR	TEAM	LVL	AGE	PA	R	2B	3B	HR	RBI	BB	K	SB	CS	AVG/OBP/SLG
2018	LAN	HI-A	23	255	44	15	3	17	43	32	65	3	1	.304/.411/.640
2018	HFD	AA	23	228	26	9	0	15	34	26	75	2	1	.231/.320/.503
2019	ABQ	AAA	24	503	77	27	0	30	105	61	141	0	1	.309/.400/.580
2020	LG	KBO	25	494	74	17	2	38	86	55	136	2	0	.278/.362/.592
2021 FS	COL	MLB	26	600	58	23	2	16	62	52	207	0	1	.207/.286/.348

Comparables: Chris Carter, Brad Eldred, Mat Gamel

It's not often that a big-league prospect (okay, fine, a *fringy* big-league prospect) will pack his bats and head overseas before reaching the show, but Ramos did just that in 2020. The timing was perfect, as smacking 38 homers and collecting half a million bucks for the pleasure sounds a lot better than getting stiffed at an alternate training site like his former Quad-A brethren. But if Ramos was hoping to parlay his time in Asia into an MLB deal, a la Eric Thames, he'll probably need to take another spin through the league. A torrid start oversells his overall line, as KBO pitchers soon found real holes in his swing and exploited his lack of bat speed. Wherever he goes, he's tracking to have Roberto Petagine's career. Perhaps he should call up Petagine—a former LG Twin himself—and ask which continent he enjoyed playing on more.

YEAR	TEAM	LVL	AGE	PA	DRC+	BABIP	BRR	FRAA	WARP
2018	LAN	HI-A	23	255	159	.364	1.2	1B(42): -0.8	1.2
2018	HFD	AA	23	228	116	.279	-1.1	1B(42): -0.4	0.2
2019	ABQ	AAA	24	503	124	.390	-1.3	1B(104): -7.8, 3B(2): -0.1	1.4
2020	LG	KBO	25	494					
2021 FS	COL	MLB	26	600	71	.305	-0.7	1B -3, 3B 0	-1.7

Brendan Rodgers 2B

Born: 08/09/96   Age: 24   Bats: R   Throws: R
Height: 6'0"   Weight: 204   Origin: Round 1, 2015 Draft (#3 overall)

YEAR	TEAM	LVL	AGE	PA	R	2B	3B	HR	RBI	BB	K	SB	CS	AVG/OBP/SLG
2018	HFD	AA	21	402	49	23	2	17	62	30	76	12	3	.275/.342/.493
2018	ABQ	AAA	21	72	5	4	0	0	5	1	16	0	0	.232/.264/.290
2019	ABQ	AAA	22	160	34	10	1	9	21	14	27	0	0	.350/.412/.622
2019	COL	MLB	22	81	8	2	0	0	7	4	27	0	0	.224/.272/.250
2020	COL	MLB	23	21	1	1	0	0	2	0	6	0	0	.095/.095/.143
2021 FS	COL	MLB	24	600	64	21	3	23	72	35	171	1	1	.231/.289/.405
2021 DC	COL	MLB	24	335	36	11	1	13	40	19	95	0	1	.231/.289/.405

Comparables: Josh Barfield, Reid Brignac, Luis Urías

After years of hype and promise, including four years in the top 20 of our prospect lists, Rodgers hasn't quite located that sweet swing that propelled him through the bush-league ranks. The 2020 numbers encompassed an 11-day stretch, which is exactly one Scaramucci, so hold it against him if you must, but the track record before that still stands. The loud contact should eventually make its way into the bat he routinely holds; however if he struggles in yet another year he may need to hire Kayleigh McEnany to write this paragraph next time.

YEAR	TEAM	LVL	AGE	PA	DRC+	BABIP	BRR	FRAA	WARP
2018	HFD	AA	21	402	113	.301	0.6	SS(58): -6.7, 2B(21): -2.1, 3B(17): 1.7	0.9
2018	ABQ	AAA	21	72	48	.302	-0.3	SS(11): -1.8, 3B(4): -0.2, 2B(3): -0.5	-0.5
2019	ABQ	AAA	22	160	130	.380	2.0	2B(27): -1.9, SS(6): -0.1, 3B(3): 0.3	1.2
2019	COL	MLB	22	81	46	.347	1.5	2B(16): 1.1, SS(9): -1.1	-0.1
2020	COL	MLB	23	21	83	.133	0.0	2B(5): -0.9, SS(1): -0.0	-0.1
2021 FS	COL	MLB	24	600	85	.293	-0.4	2B -2, SS -1	0.3
2021 DC	COL	MLB	24	335	85	.293	-0.2	2B -1, SS -1	0.2

Colorado Rockies 2021

Drew Romo C
Born: 08/29/01 Age: 19 Bats: S Throws: R
Height: 6'1" Weight: 205 Origin: Round 1, 2020 Draft (#35 overall)

Romo is the first high school catcher taken in the first round since Joe Mauer who played on consecutive under-18 Team USA teams. Any lingering correlation, however, will fail to include the former Twins MVP's sideburns. His foremost skills reside in squatting and sticking a glove in front of his face, and having the sort of body shape that led someone to suggest catching in the first place. And as with all highly-ranked catching prospects, he comes with the usual assortment of praise for intangibles pre-installed. Still, it's the burgeoning promise in standing upright and holding manufactured timber products that tempted the Rockies into using their first-round competitive balance pick on him.

Aaron Schunk 3B
Born: 07/24/97 Age: 23 Bats: R Throws: R
Height: 6'2" Weight: 205 Origin: Round 2, 2019 Draft (#62 overall)

YEAR	TEAM	LVL	AGE	PA	R	2B	3B	HR	RBI	BB	K	SB	CS	AVG/OBP/SLG
2019	BOI	SS	21	192	31	12	2	6	23	14	25	4	1	.306/.370/.503
2021 FS	COL	MLB	23	600	54	24	3	12	59	38	144	5	2	.226/.283/.350

Comparables: Matt Skole, Gaby Sanchez, J.D. Davis

Schunk, a second or possibly third baseman, is constantly turning heads in the minor leagues. Possibly because of the bat, but mostly because his last name is being said and people are wondering what that sound is.

YEAR	TEAM	LVL	AGE	PA	DRC+	BABIP	BRR	FRAA	WARP
2019	BOI	SS	21	192	138	.329	1.8	3B(37): 7.4	2.2
2021 FS	COL	MLB	23	600	75	.283	0.1	3B 13	0.5

Michael Toglia 1B
Born: 08/16/98   Age: 22   Bats: S   Throws: L
Height: 6'5"   Weight: 226   Origin: Round 1, 2019 Draft (#23 overall)

YEAR	TEAM	LVL	AGE	PA	R	2B	3B	HR	RBI	BB	K	SB	CS	AVG/OBP/SLG
2019	BOI	SS	20	176	25	7	0	9	26	28	45	1	1	.248/.369/.483
2021 FS	COL	MLB	22	600	48	21	2	11	53	42	209	1	1	.190/.252/.299

Comparables: Shane Peterson, Joe Mahoney, Ali Solis

Despite registering nary a stat, Toglia got some reps at the fabled alternate site last summer to prepare for an exciting career in professional first base management. He remains an athletic defender by first-base standards and an extremely promising hitter except by first-base standards.

YEAR	TEAM	LVL	AGE	PA	DRC+	BABIP	BRR	FRAA	WARP
2019	BOI	SS	20	176	131	.290	0.3	1B(38): -0.2	0.6
2021 FS	COL	MLB	22	600	52	.283	-0.5	1B 0	-2.9

Zac Veen OF
Born: 12/12/01   Age: 19   Bats: L   Throws: R
Height: 6'4"   Weight: 190   Origin: Round 1, 2020 Draft (#9 overall)

While everybody in 2020 was waiting for a vaccine, the Colorado Rockies waited until the ninth-overall pick in the amateur draft for a Zac Veen. As a high school outfielder, he may take just as much time to go through clinical phases before he's completely inoculated from the horrors of major league curveballs and pinpoint command. His 6'4" frame should help him develop decent power, but may in turn scooch him into a corner outfield spot. Veen is the first outfielder taken by Colorado in the first round since David Dahl, and both were out of high school and bat left-handed. Veen is more well-rounded than the offense-leaning Dahl, and should he start developing similar power, we can only hope that Veen home runs will be called "flew shots."

Colorado Rockies 2021

Ryan Vilade SS
Born: 02/18/99 Age: 22 Bats: R Throws: R
Height: 6'2" Weight: 226 Origin: Round 2, 2017 Draft (#48 overall)

YEAR	TEAM	LVL	AGE	PA	R	2B	3B	HR	RBI	BB	K	SB	CS	AVG/OBP/SLG
2018	ASH	LO-A	19	533	77	20	4	5	44	49	96	17	13	.274/.353/.368
2019	LAN	HI-A	20	587	92	27	10	12	71	56	94	24	7	.303/.367/.466
2021 FS	COL	MLB	22	600	52	23	4	8	53	50	157	9	6	.225/.295/.335

Comparables: Tyler Wade, Amed Rosario, Yolmer Sánchez

Vilade went from a promising offensive-leaning shortstop to a promising offensive-leaning third baseman last spring. If he leans any more he'll be in foul territory, so he should knock it off.

YEAR	TEAM	LVL	AGE	PA	DRC+	BABIP	BRR	FRAA	WARP
2018	ASH	LO-A	19	533	112	.333	-1.9	SS(116): -6.3	1.1
2019	LAN	HI-A	20	587	118	.341	2.5	SS(83): -4.0, 3B(46): -4.3	2.6
2021 FS	COL	MLB	22	600	74	.301	0.8	SS -3, 3B -2	-0.7

Colton Welker 3B
Born: 10/09/97 Age: 23 Bats: R Throws: R
Height: 6'1" Weight: 235 Origin: Round 4, 2016 Draft (#110 overall)

YEAR	TEAM	LVL	AGE	PA	R	2B	3B	HR	RBI	BB	K	SB	CS	AVG/OBP/SLG
2018	LAN	HI-A	20	509	74	32	0	13	82	42	103	5	1	.333/.383/.489
2019	HFD	AA	21	394	37	23	1	10	53	32	68	2	1	.252/.313/.408
2021 FS	COL	MLB	23	600	66	24	2	15	64	38	146	3	2	.240/.295/.378
2021 DC	COL	MLB	23	192	21	7	0	5	20	12	46	0	1	.240/.295/.378

Comparables: Matt Dominguez, Lonnie Chisenhall, Andy LaRoche

The great sieve known as "pitchers with better stuff" has diminished corner infielder **Colton Welker**'s power profile. Despite the holes in the swing, he's pretty good at the other two true outcomes. Fortunately, when a prospect is blocked by someone like Nolan Arenado, they have all the time they need—maybe if Welker waits long enough, the game will change enough to outlaw balls in play entirely.

YEAR	TEAM	LVL	AGE	PA	DRC+	BABIP	BRR	FRAA	WARP
2018	LAN	HI-A	20	509	139	.395	1.1	3B(92): -9.3, 1B(6): -0.7	1.2
2019	HFD	AA	21	394	112	.281	-2.8	3B(63): -1.5, 1B(27): 2.2	1.3
2021 FS	COL	MLB	23	600	82	.299	-0.3	3B -4, 1B 2	-0.6
2021 DC	COL	MLB	23	192	82	.299	-0.1	3B -1, 1B 1	-0.2

Ben Bowden LHP

Born: 10/21/94 Age: 26 Bats: L Throws: L
Height: 6'4" Weight: 249 Origin: Round 2, 2016 Draft (#45 overall)

YEAR	TEAM	LVL	AGE	W	L	SV	G	GS	IP	H	HR	BB/9	K/9	K	GB%	BABIP
2018	ASH	LO-A	23	3	0	0	15	0	15^1	17	2	2.9	14.7	25	43.2%	.429
2018	LAN	HI-A	23	4	2	0	34	0	36^2	35	6	3.7	13.0	53	31.5%	.341
2019	HFD	AA	24	0	0	20	26	0	25^2	8	1	2.5	14.7	42	33.3%	.175
2019	ABQ	AAA	24	1	3	1	22	0	26	29	4	5.9	12.8	37	34.3%	.379
2021 FS	*COL*	*MLB*	*26*	*2*	*2*	*0*	*57*	*0*	*50*	*42*	*7*	*4.9*	*11.2*	*62*	*36.5%*	*.293*
2021 DC	*COL*	*MLB*	*26*	*1*	*1*	*0*	*32*	*0*	*29*	*24*	*4*	*4.9*	*11.2*	*36*	*36.5%*	*.293*

Comparables: Ryan Burr, Yohan Ramirez, Caleb Frare

Throwing ridiculously hard as a lefty out of college with command is a surefire way to scoot through the minors, but Bowden, a 2016 draftee, has been dinged by injuries here and there. Maybe this year, though. Most assessors agree on what he is: a guy who can challenge hitters with his fastball, and when that's not working, challenge them with a fastball. The disparity is more about how much to care about lefty relievers. Get as excited as you deem fit.

YEAR	TEAM	LVL	AGE	WHIP	ERA	DRA-	WARP	MPH	FB%	WHF	CSP
2018	ASH	LO-A	23	1.43	3.52	67	0.3				
2018	LAN	HI-A	23	1.36	4.17	93	0.1				
2019	HFD	AA	24	0.58	1.05	39	0.8				
2019	ABQ	AAA	24	1.77	5.88	92	0.4				
2021 FS	*COL*	*MLB*	*26*	*1.39*	*4.28*	*97*	*0.3*				
2021 DC	*COL*	*MLB*	*26*	*1.39*	*4.28*	*97*	*0.2*				

Colorado Rockies 2021

Phillip Diehl LHP
Born: 07/16/94 Age: 26 Bats: L Throws: L
Height: 6'2" Weight: 169 Origin: Round 27, 2016 Draft (#818 overall)

YEAR	TEAM	LVL	AGE	W	L	SV	G	GS	IP	H	HR	BB/9	K/9	K	GB%	BABIP
2018	TAM	HI-A	23	2	2	3	25	0	48²	37	2	2.2	14.6	79	42.0%	.357
2018	TRN	AA	23	0	1	1	14	0	26²	18	2	3.7	9.8	29	33.8%	.254
2019	HFD	AA	24	0	0	0	11	0	13¹	5	0	2.0	8.1	12	58.1%	.161
2019	ABQ	AAA	24	2	1	0	39	0	45¹	54	16	3.0	10.3	52	36.2%	.333
2019	COL	MLB	24	0	0	0	10	0	7¹	10	1	2.5	9.8	8	20.8%	.391
2020	COL	MLB	25	0	0	0	6	0	6	7	2	1.5	6.0	4	45.0%	.278
2021 FS	COL	MLB	26	2	2	0	57	0	50	47	8	3.6	9.4	52	37.5%	.295
2021 DC	COL	MLB	26	1	1	0	32	0	29	27	5	3.6	9.4	30	37.5%	.295

Comparables: Travis Bergen, Trevor Kelley, James Pazos

Our advanced pitching numbers noticeably temper the small sample shellacking that put control artist Diehl's 2020 ERA into double digits. This is why DRA stands for Denver Redemption Algorithms.

YEAR	TEAM	LVL	AGE	WHIP	ERA	DRA-	WARP	MPH	FB%	WHF	CSP
2018	TAM	HI-A	23	1.01	3.14	48	1.5				
2018	TRN	AA	23	1.09	1.35	53	0.8				
2019	HFD	AA	24	0.60	0.00	59	0.3				
2019	ABQ	AAA	24	1.52	6.75	127	0.0				
2019	COL	MLB	24	1.64	7.36	128	-0.1	91.7	44.9%	37.9%	
2020	COL	MLB	25	1.33	10.50	95	0.1	91.2	55.2%	16.3%	
2021 FS	COL	MLB	26	1.36	4.57	101	0.2	91.4	50.6%	25.9%	42.9%
2021 DC	COL	MLB	26	1.36	4.57	101	0.1	91.4	50.6%	25.9%	42.9%

Peter Lambert RHP
Born: 04/18/97 Age: 24 Bats: R Throws: R
Height: 6'2" Weight: 208 Origin: Round 2, 2015 Draft (#44 overall)

YEAR	TEAM	LVL	AGE	W	L	SV	G	GS	IP	H	HR	BB/9	K/9	K	GB%	BABIP
2018	HFD	AA	21	8	2	0	15	15	92²	80	6	1.2	7.3	75	48.9%	.285
2018	ABQ	AAA	21	2	5	0	11	11	55¹	72	5	2.4	5.0	31	50.3%	.349
2019	ABQ	AAA	22	2	2	0	11	11	60¹	63	10	2.4	7.6	51	52.6%	.294
2019	COL	MLB	22	3	7	0	19	19	89¹	119	18	3.6	5.7	57	46.1%	.338
2021 FS	COL	MLB	24	9	9	0	26	26	150	160	25	3.2	6.6	110	46.8%	.298
2021 DC	COL	MLB	24	2	2	0	9	8	32.3	34	5	3.2	6.6	23	46.8%	.298

Comparables: Jake Thompson, Zach Eflin, Jaime Barria

A lambert is a unit of measurement used to convey the luminance of light. A Peter Lambert is a unit that underwent Tommy John surgery last summer and won't burn brightly until 2022.

YEAR	TEAM	LVL	AGE	WHIP	ERA	DRA-	WARP	MPH	FB%	WHF	CSP
2018	HFD	AA	21	0.99	2.23	96	0.9				
2018	ABQ	AAA	21	1.57	5.04	100	0.5				
2019	ABQ	AAA	22	1.31	5.07	65	2.1				
2019	COL	MLB	22	1.74	7.25	152	-1.6	94.3	53.0%	16.8%	
2021 FS	COL	MLB	24	1.43	4.98	109	0.7	94.3	53.0%	16.8%	47.0%
2021 DC	COL	MLB	24	1.43	4.98	109	0.1	94.3	53.0%	16.8%	47.0%

Scott Oberg RHP
Born: 03/13/90 Age: 31 Bats: R Throws: R
Height: 6'2" Weight: 207 Origin: Round 15, 2012 Draft (#468 overall)

YEAR	TEAM	LVL	AGE	W	L	SV	G	GS	IP	H	HR	BB/9	K/9	K	GB%	BABIP
2018	ABQ	AAA	28	1	0	3	13	0	15^1	14	1	1.2	8.2	14	60.0%	.342
2018	COL	MLB	28	8	1	0	56	0	58^2	45	4	1.8	8.7	57	57.7%	.270
2019	COL	MLB	29	6	1	5	49	0	56	39	5	3.7	9.2	57	49.3%	.246
2021 FS	COL	MLB	31	2	2	6	57	0	50	44	5	3.0	9.3	51	51.3%	.296
2021 DC	COL	MLB	31	1	1	6	38	0	40.7	36	4	3.0	9.3	42	51.3%	.296

Comparables: Shawn Armstrong, Nick Wittgren, Emilio Pagán

You may be surprised to learn Oberg is fourth all-time in Rockies history in pitching win probability added, but then again you may not be, because it's a list of Rockies pitchers and things always get weird after the first couple names. The injury-addled setup man built up a reputation out of reliability, so his absence was felt last year when blood clots ravaged his body for the third time, wiping out his entire 2020. He's under contract through '22, a reward for his understated dominance; given that there are so many more weird Rockies lists for him to ascend, this could just be the tip of the Oberg.

YEAR	TEAM	LVL	AGE	WHIP	ERA	DRA-	WARP	MPH	FB%	WHF	CSP
2018	ABQ	AAA	28	1.04	1.76	86	0.2				
2018	COL	MLB	28	0.97	2.45	77	1.0	97.0	55.1%	27.9%	
2019	COL	MLB	29	1.11	2.25	67	1.2	96.0	52.2%	27.9%	
2021 FS	COL	MLB	31	1.23	3.48	81	0.8	96.3	53.2%	27.9%	47.6%
2021 DC	COL	MLB	31	1.23	3.48	81	0.6	96.3	53.2%	27.9%	47.6%

AJ Ramos RHP
Born: 09/20/86 Age: 34 Bats: R Throws: R
Height: 5'10" Weight: 200 Origin: Round 21, 2009 Draft (#638 overall)

YEAR	TEAM	LVL	AGE	W	L	SV	G	GS	IP	H	HR	BB/9	K/9	K	GB%	BABIP
2018	NYM	MLB	31	2	2	0	28	0	19^2	17	3	6.9	10.1	22	27.5%	.292
2020	COL	MLB	33	0	0	0	3	0	2^2	4	1	10.1	3.4	1	18.2%	.300
2021 FS	COL	MLB	34	2	3	0	57	0	50	46	8	5.5	9.2	50	36.1%	.290

Comparables: Michael Gonzalez, Pedro Strop, Brad Brach

Colorado Rockies 2021

Ramos would have been the biggest comeback story in the Rockies bullpen, if Daniel Bard hadn't landed his 99.99th-percentile outcome. An All-Star five years ago, the former electric Marlins and incandescent Mets closer recovered from torn labrum surgery, missing over two calendar years of organized baseball. Announcing a comeback in the summer was a bold gambit, given that MLB was trying to do the same thing. After coming up lame on deals with the Dodgers and Cubs, the Rockies ultimately gave him a few innings in the final week. His stuff was never blow-away, but rather move-enough to create missed swings, but in the teensy 2020 sample he most certainly did not do that. It's always nice to have someone that has a 40-save season in your ranks, though you'd prefer those saves didn't predate the Trump Administration.

YEAR	TEAM	LVL	AGE	WHIP	ERA	DRA-	WARP	MPH	FB%	WHF	CSP
2018	NYM	MLB	31	1.63	6.41	87	0.2	94.1	36.7%	29.1%	
2020	COL	MLB	33	2.62	3.38	150	0.0	93.4	33.3%	16.1%	
2021 FS	COL	MLB	34	1.55	5.19	110	0.0	93.9	35.5%	24.5%	44.7%

Ryan Rolison   LHP
Born: 07/11/97   Age: 23   Bats: R   Throws: L
Height: 6'2"   Weight: 213   Origin: Round 1, 2018 Draft (#22 overall)

YEAR	TEAM	LVL	AGE	W	L	SV	G	GS	IP	H	HR	BB/9	K/9	K	GB%	BABIP
2018	GJ	ROK	20	0	1	0	9	9	29	15	2	2.5	10.6	34	65.7%	.200
2019	ASH	LO-A	21	2	1	0	3	3	14^2	8	0	1.2	8.6	14	37.8%	.216
2019	LAN	HI-A	21	6	7	0	22	22	116^1	129	22	2.9	9.1	118	43.6%	.327
2021 FS	COL	MLB	23	2	3	0	57	0	50	49	8	3.9	7.9	43	43.1%	.290
2021 DC	COL	MLB	23	1	1	0	4	4	21.7	21	3	3.9	7.9	19	43.1%	.290

Comparables: Braxton Garrett, Kris Bubic, Patrick Sandoval

There are fewer cursed accolades than "top Rockies pitching prospect," but at least Rolison isn't being considered for Spinal Tap's next drummer. The team actually considered promoting him for the stretch run, given that they lacked a lefty reliever and Rolison sports the quality fastball-slider combo for the gig. Instead, he'll begin the season in Double-A trying not to think about how his curveball will behave in Coors. Then again, he might still be better off in Colorado than, say, Tampa Bay, where he wouldn't make their Top-10 list unless it went to 11.

YEAR	TEAM	LVL	AGE	WHIP	ERA	DRA-	WARP	MPH	FB%	WHF	CSP
2018	GJ	ROK	20	0.79	1.86						
2019	ASH	LO-A	21	0.68	0.61	49	0.5				
2019	LAN	HI-A	21	1.44	4.87	94	0.6				
2021 FS	COL	MLB	23	1.43	4.79	108	0.0				
2021 DC	COL	MLB	23	1.43	4.79	108	0.1				

Antonio Santos   RHP

Born: 10/06/96   Age: 24   Bats: R   Throws: R
Height: 6'3"   Weight: 223   Origin: International Free Agent, 2015

YEAR	TEAM	LVL	AGE	W	L	SV	G	GS	IP	H	HR	BB/9	K/9	K	GB%	BABIP
2018	ASH	LO-A	21	1	10	0	15	15	86^1	100	8	1.3	9.0	86	50.7%	.355
2018	LAN	HI-A	21	4	3	0	12	12	65^2	74	15	2.9	7.7	56	37.0%	.303
2019	LAN	HI-A	22	3	6	0	18	18	99^1	116	11	1.6	8.7	96	39.3%	.349
2019	HFD	AA	22	3	3	0	8	8	45^2	47	3	2.0	8.7	44	38.2%	.338
2020	COL	MLB	23	0	1	0	3	1	6	14	1	6.0	6.0	4	36.0%	.542
2021 FS	*COL*	*MLB*	*24*	*2*	*3*	*0*	*57*	*0*	*50*	*53*	*9*	*2.6*	*6.9*	*38*	*38.2%*	*.296*
2021 DC	*COL*	*MLB*	*24*	*1*	*1*	*0*	*21*	*0*	*17.3*	*18*	*3*	*2.6*	*6.9*	*13*	*38.2%*	*.296*

Comparables: Chase De Jong, Randy Rosario, Blake Snell

Santos was rinsed in his first few outings, but he has an out pitch, he's got it around here somewhere, just give him a minute or so, we are going to love it when we see it, please hold, thank you for your patience.

YEAR	TEAM	LVL	AGE	WHIP	ERA	DRA-	WARP	MPH	FB%	WHF	CSP
2018	ASH	LO-A	21	1.30	4.48	80	1.4				
2018	LAN	HI-A	21	1.45	5.21	158	-1.9				
2019	LAN	HI-A	22	1.35	4.35	106	-0.2				
2019	HFD	AA	22	1.25	4.93	104	-0.1				
2020	COL	MLB	23	3.00	16.50	140	-0.1	95.7	59.4%	11.7%	
2021 FS	*COL*	*MLB*	*24*	*1.36*	*4.95*	*110*	*0.0*	*95.7*	*59.4%*	*11.7%*	*45.7%*
2021 DC	*COL*	*MLB*	*24*	*1.36*	*4.95*	*110*	*0.0*	*95.7*	*59.4%*	*11.7%*	*45.7%*

Henry Sosa RHP

Born: 07/28/85 Age: 35 Bats: R Throws: R
Height: 6'1" Weight: 210 Origin:

YEAR	TEAM	LVL	AGE	W	L	SV	G	GS	IP	H	HR	BB/9	K/9	K	GB%	BABIP
2018	LG	KBO	32	9	9	0	27	27	181^1	192	16	1.0	9.0	181		
2019	FUB	CPBL	33	8	2	0	12	12	86^2	60	5	1.0	8.8	85		
2019	SK	KBO	33	9	3	0	16	16	94^1	85	15	2.0	9.2	96		
2020	FUB	CPBL	34	15	5	0	29	29	194^1	230	12	1.7	8.0	172		
2021									No projection							

You might remember Sosa from a lifetime or two ago, when he was a well-regarded prospect for the Giants (and earned himself a handful of mentions in BP Annuals of yesteryear). While he did briefly reach The Show on a miserable Astros team in 2011, Sosa's career is mostly defined by his fine work overseas, first in the KBO for much of the 2010s, and now in the CPBL. He joined the Guardians in 2019, but then returned to the KBO under some duress, as Korea had changed its income tax laws in 2015, and teams failed to notify players of the repercussions. Sosa found himself owing a signficant sum in back taxes, so his signing bonus paid off what he owed. He was glad to get back to Taiwan in 2020. Awarded the league's Pitcher of the Month award last September, the hard-throwing Sosa was the anchor of a resurgent Guardians team that played well down the stretch after a rough first half of the year. The Guardians weren't shy about relying on Sosa; his four complete games were the most in the league (only one other pitcher, Esmil Rogers, had as many as two), and he was also the league-leader in games started and innings pitched.

YEAR	TEAM	LVL	AGE	WHIP	ERA	DRA-	WARP	MPH	FB%	WHF	CSP
2018	LG	KBO	32	1.21	3.52						
2019	FUB	CPBL	33	0.81	1.56						
2019	SK	KBO	33	1.14	3.82						
2020	FUB	CPBL	34	1.37	3.38						
2021					No projection						

Jesus Tinoco RHP

Born: 04/30/95 Age: 26 Bats: R Throws: R
Height: 6'4" Weight: 258 Origin: International Free Agent, 2011

YEAR	TEAM	LVL	AGE	W	L	SV	G	GS	IP	H	HR	BB/9	K/9	K	GB%	BABIP
2018	HFD	AA	23	9	12	0	26	26	141	149	23	2.4	8.4	132	37.6%	.315
2019	ABQ	AAA	24	3	1	1	29	0	34	33	4	4.8	6.1	23	56.2%	.287
2019	COL	MLB	24	0	3	1	24	0	36	36	12	5.5	7.0	28	43.6%	.245
2020	COL	MLB	25	0	0	0	6	0	8^2	3	0	7.3	6.2	6	78.9%	.158
2021 FS	COL	MLB	26	2	3	0	57	0	50	50	7	4.7	7.3	40	45.7%	.290

Comparables: Chase De Jong, Corey Oswalt, Keury Mella

Tinoco has a lively fastball and a decent curve but has trouble finding the strike zone. Then again, Colorado traded him to Miami only to claim him back a month later, so his own team has trouble locating *him*.

YEAR	TEAM	LVL	AGE	WHIP	ERA	DRA-	WARP	MPH	FB%	WHF	CSP
2018	HFD	AA	23	1.33	4.79	89	1.8				
2019	ABQ	AAA	24	1.50	3.97	85	0.7				
2019	COL	MLB	24	1.61	4.75	140	-0.6	96.0	62.3%	22.4%	
2020	COL	MLB	25	1.15	1.04	83	0.2	95.7	68.1%	24.6%	
2021 FS	*COL*	*MLB*	*26*	*1.53*	*5.06*	*109*	*0.0*	*95.9*	*63.8%*	*23.0%*	*42.0%*

Rockies Prospects

The State of the System:
I've rewritten this four or five times now because I thought it was too mean. It's not a good system.

The Top Ten:

★ ★ ★ *2021 Top 101 Prospect* **#49** ★ ★ ★

1
Zac Veen   OF   OFP: 60   ETA: Late 2024
Born: 12/12/01   Age: 19   Bats: L   Throws: R   Height: 6'4"   Weight: 190
Origin: Round 1, 2020 Draft (#9 overall)

The Report: After solid showings in last summer's high school all-star games, Veen's momentum continued into the fall and brief spring season, and he garnered mentions as a possible top-5 pick. It was a minor coup for the Rockies that he was still available at the ninth slot, where he was clearly the best player on the board. The smooth-swinging lefty has an advanced approach for his age, knowing when to be aggressive and when to be patient, and can do significant damage when ahead in the count. He's also more athletic than he's given credit for; his long limbs and long strides are surprisingly quick, allowing for plus speed on the basepaths and gap-to-gap coverage in the outfield. The so-so arm and likelihood he eventually loses a step probably paints him into a corner outfield spot in the future.

Development Track: Living on Florida's Atlantic coast, Veen was able to get more game action than almost any other high profile prospect prior to the shutdown thanks to the area's early start and preseason tournaments. There is room for growth on his frame, although keeping him light on his feet to maintain his athleticism would be ideal over bulky muscle. The bat looked as advertised at instructs, but his defense will need some work. With patience, one day he could terrorize opposing pitchers at Coors Field.

Variance: Medium. All the pieces are there to accommodate a modest floor while also including an All-Star potential ceiling.

J.P. Breen's Fantasy Take: Top-end bats in Colorado's system will always be overvalued, due to the #CoorsEffect. Veen, however, might be worth the lofty price tag. His advanced approach at the plate and his feel for hitting give him an attractive dynasty floor, whether with the Rockies or elsewhere, and the power-speed potential could make him fantasy stud. His pure upside is the highest of anyone selected in the 2020 MLB Draft.

2. Ryan Rolison   LHP   OFP: 55   ETA: Late 2021/Early 2022
Born: 07/11/97   Age: 23   Bats: R   Throws: L   Height: 6'2"   Weight: 213
Origin: Round 1, 2018 Draft (#22 overall)

The Report: Given the Rockies' early competitiveness in the truncated season, there were whispers of bringing up Rolison for the stretch run. They were operating without a left-handed reliever in the bullpen for the majority of the year, not that James Pazos or Phillip Diehl inspired much confidence in the first place. Colorado ultimately didn't make the call, but it wasn't for a lack of success and stuff as Rolison showed an improved fastball and a sharper slider than before. The two-pitch mix ran through his teammates at the alternate site while Rolison showed improved strike-throwing ability.

Development Track: The Rockies are committed to developing Rolison as a starter, hence why they did not want him to work out of a bullpen without a clear spot for a starting pitcher. He will start 2021 on Double-A team "TBD" and most likely spend the whole season there. The Rockies hardly put guys on the fast track, even the advanced college picks who are supposed to move quickly.

Variance: Medium. Coors Field hasn't exactly been kind to pitchers without premium velocity, or to players who rely on their curveball as an out pitch (see Hoffman, Jeff).

J.P. Breen's Fantasy Take: While too many dynasty owners overestimate the #CoorsEffect for batters, I don't believe that's true on the pitching side. Dynasty owners tend to shy away from Rockies pitching prospects, and they should. Rolison is no different. At the absolute best, he's a mid-rotation arm who can strike out a batter per inning, thanks to his curveball, but even that is an undesirable profile at Coors. Even worse, Rolison is a fly-ball pitcher who had home-run issues in High-A. He's not a Top-300 dynasty prospect for me, though he'd be more interesting with a different organization.

3. Ryan Vilade   SS   OFP: 50   ETA: 2022
Born: 02/18/99   Age: 22   Bats: R   Throws: R   Height: 6'2"   Weight: 226
Origin: Round 2, 2017 Draft (#48 overall)

The Report: Going into 2020, Vilade was prepared to play the outfield for the first time. It wasn't going to work as a shortstop, although we felt the Rockies may have given him more leash as a third baseman given his relative inexperience there before the 2019 season. There is much less uncertainty about Vilade at the plate, as he uses the whole field, doesn't strikeout often, and can put a charge into baseballs. Given the large dimensions of Coors Field, expect to see a lot of extra-base hits. But he keeps moving down the defensive spectrum, putting more pressure on the bat to perform.

Development Track: Vilade hasn't faced Double-A pitching yet. He will have to do that next year while playing a new position. Coors Field isn't exactly small, and being a below-average runner might be an issue even in the corners.

Variance: High. Vilade is learning a new position, hasn't faced advanced pitching yet, and had a notable split between Lancaster and everywhere else.

J.P. Breen's Fantasy Take: I am cooler on Vilade than most dynasty experts. He stole 17 bases in 2018 and 24 bases in 2019, but the 21-year-old doesn't profile to be a league-average runner. He'll be hard-pressed to reach double-digit steals, especially since his minor-league success rates have been very poor. Vilade reportedly has significant power potential; however, he has yet to post an ISO over .200 as a professional. He's a fringe top-200 prospect who will need to hit for major power to be fantasy relevant whatsoever in shallow leagues.

4. Michael Toglia 1B   OFP: 50   ETA: 2023
Born: 08/16/98 Age: 22 Bats: S Throws: L Height: 6'5" Weight: 226
Origin: Round 1, 2019 Draft (#23 overall)

The Report: Toglia is a switch-hitter with plus power. He can drive the ball all over, but the swing-and-miss became more of an issue as he transitioned from college to the pros. Three true outcome hitters don't typically rank high on a team prospect list, especially when they are playing mostly first base. The defense there is plus, at least, and he is athletic enough that they will give him opportunities in the outfield to add some versatility.

Development Track: The lack of a 2020 season—where you would have hoped for his advanced college bat to power its way to Double-A—leaves us without answers to just how much the big pop will play in games against better competition. Toglia will have to wait for 2021 to make his full-season debut, which will likely be in a less hitter-friendly park than Lancaster's. He will move through first base and the two outfield corners, but wherever he stands he will have to tighten up the plate discipline to project for long term impact with the bat.

Variance: Medium. While Toglia's pro resume is short, he does show quality game power already and good defense at first base, which gives him a higher floor than other three true outcome types.

J.P. Breen's Fantasy Take: Toglia is a good example of why defense matters in dynasty formats. Without a good glove, Toglia is a low-average power hitter who needs to absolutely mash to reach the majors in any capacity. With his good first-base defense, there are multiple paths available to fantasy relevance. The 2021 season will give us a better idea as to whether he's truly a drag in terms of batting average. Toglia is a top-150 dynasty prospect, better than Vilade thanks to role certainty and better current power.

Colorado Rockies 2021

5 **Chris McMahon** OFP: 50 ETA: 2023
Born: 02/04/99 Age: 22 Bats: R Throws: R Height: 6'2" Weight: 217
Origin: Round 2, 2020 Draft (#46 overall)

The Report: Among the top performers for last year's Collegiate National Team, McMahon was finally healthy and showing stuff area scouts believed was first-round caliber. After leading the team in strikeouts, he came out in fall workouts up to 98 mph and dominated in his few spring starts. Had the NCAA season continued, it's possible he could have worked his way further up draft boards in what was an incredibly deep college pitching class. The delivery is consistent, staying a hair upright and tall on his front leg without pushing off much with his back hip. So his mid-90s fastball is rooted in arm strength with the potential to add a tick or two with more lower half engagement. The breaking ball is a slurvy, downer-type that flashes good movement as a chase pitch even though it can be inconsistent.

Development Track: Staying healthy has been the issue during McMahon's amateur career. He has solid tools as a starting pitcher, needing sustained reps to work on his secondaries, including a changeup that has improved over time. Between the stout body, mechanics, and lack of mileage on his arm, there is some hope that there is a lot of projection left to be tapped into.

Variance: High. You just want to see more of what was on display in his four starts at The U this spring, but there's also the chance he could be a mid-rotation piece if all goes well.

J.P. Breen's Fantasy Take: Projectable collegiate pitchers are always intriguing, but the combination of health issues and inconsistent secondary stuff takes away most of that shine. Of course, there's also the Coors thing. The upside isn't high enough to warrant drafting in your offseason supplemental drafts, and he didn't even make the Honorable Mentions in Bret and Jesse's recap of the top-40 dynasty prospects from the 2020 MLB Draft.

6 **Aaron Schunk** 3B OFP: 50 ETA: Late 2022
Born: 07/24/97 Age: 23 Bats: R Throws: R Height: 6'2" Weight: 205
Origin: Round 2, 2019 Draft (#62 overall)

The Report: Schunk had a power spike his junior year at Georgia which jumped him into the second round of the draft. The ball continued to fly off his bat in the friendly confines of Boise, and the power is the most likely tool to reach above-average. The rest of the scouting report is a 45 or 50. Schunk has all the physical tools to be average at the hot corner, and might be athletic enough to play some second as well, which is the kind of infield positional flexibility the Rockies like to develop. There's not a long track record of the kind of power you'd want from an everyday third baseman, though.

Development Track: Schunk got some 2020 reps in at instructs and the profile looked more or less the same. He was on the older side for a college draftee and will turn 24 in the middle of the 2021 season, so you'd like to see him hit the ground running.

Variance: Medium. There's a broad base of potentially average tools, so between that and potential flexibility to move around the infield, Schunk should get major league reps. For example, Colorado gave Pat Valaika 400+ PAs across four seasons. But like Toglia, the missing year of mashing full-season ball injects some uncertainty.

J.P. Breen's Fantasy Take: Oof, it's never a great sign, at least in terms of dynasty value, when Pat Valaika appears in your write-up. Schunk hit .306/.370/.503 in 2019, but that came in the NWL and he was an experienced college bat. That stat line doesn't tell us much. Maybe he's a utility bat who hits 15-20 homers with a decent average, but that ain't worth more than a wait-and-see approach.

7 Brenton Doyle RF   OFP: 50   ETA: 2023
Born: 05/14/98   Age: 23   Bats: R   Throws: R   Height: 6'3"   Weight: 200
Origin: Round 4, 2019 Draft (#129 overall)

The Report: Doyle was a potential breakout prospect for 2020. He has tools, athleticism, physicality, and a relatively inexperienced background to make it all dangerous enough to cause trouble. He still has all that, and we are moving him up based on the upside he offers relative to other players who lack those tools. Everything you want he has: power, arm strength, above-average speed, outfield instincts; he just has not been consistently tested against better players yet.

Development Track: Doyle may start off in Low-A "TBD" in 2021, but could move quickly onward to stiffer competition if he sets it ablaze. He needs the repetitions.

Variance: High. D2 background, only one short season of pro experience (albeit very good), missing a year of games and experience.

J.P. Breen's Fantasy Take: >Doyle is the unheralded gem of this system. He's a potential everyday outfielder with five-category production, and those are difficult to find outside the top-250 dynasty prospects. Doyle may not make keeper cuts this winter in deep leagues—and is likely unrostered in shallower leagues—and is a sneaky target for supplemental drafts. He's a strong half-season away from being a dynasty darling.

8 Colton Welker 3B   OFP: 50   ETA: Late 2021/Early 2022
Born: 10/09/97   Age: 23   Bats: R   Throws: R   Height: 6'1"   Weight: 235
Origin: Round 4, 2016 Draft (#110 overall)

Colorado Rockies 2021

The Report: Welker hit his first professional speed bump in 2019. He got off to a hot start in Hartford, but his aggressive, pull-and-lift approach got exposed as the season went on, and he struggled to adjust to Double-A arms who could move their fastball around the zone and break off quality secondaries in hitter's counts. Welker doesn't get cheated up there, and anything he squares is a threat to go for extra base hits, but he will need to tone down the aggressiveness and find a balance to his approach for the plus raw to get into games enough to carry a corner infield profile. He's a better fit at first than third, as the range and arm are a little light for the hot corner at times. He moves well laterally despite a sturdy frame, so maybe they will try him at second too.

Development Track: Welker spent the summer at the Rockies' alternate site and likely never had much of a chance to break into a crowded major league corner infield situation. That might open up some with a potential Nolan Arenado trade, but he could use some consolidation time in Triple-A Albuquerque or whatever their affiliate is in 2021. I'm sure Major League Baseball will let us all know at some point.

Variance: Medium. Welker's approach and defensive limitations could make him more of a short-side platoon bench piece.

J.P. Breen's Fantasy Take: Welker lacks a carrying fantasy tool. Scouting reports have long talked about his power potential, but he hasn't posted an ISO over .162 in his professional career. Plus, his average took a step backward against more advanced pitching. If we're talking about a potential platoon bat, as mentioned above, we're talking about dynasty irrelevance. He's not a top-300 dynasty prospect for me.

9   Drew Romo   C   OFP: 50   ETA: 2025
Born: 08/29/01   Age: 19   Bats: S   Throws: R   Height: 6'1"   Weight: 205
Origin: Round 1, 2020 Draft (#35 overall)

The Report: One Texas area scout said of Romo that he was the best defensive backstop to come out of high school in the last 20 years. High praise, considering the position has been notoriously difficult to draft and develop without players first going to college. As expected, he receives excellent grades with the glove and the arm while the offensive marks are decidedly behind. There is some thump in the bat, more from the right side as a switch-hitter, as both strokes tend to get slightly disconnected and need greater consistency.

Development Track: Romo's deficiencies are correctable, that is the good news. The two hardest skill-sets to master in baseball are switch-hitting and everything that encompasses the catcher position. In trying to do both, he has a very tall task ahead of him.

Variance: Very High. The list of successful catchers drafted out of high school in recent memory is miniscule. If he only maintains what he can do behind the plate, the bar is set so low as a hitter nowadays it won't take much to clear it.

J.P. Breen's Fantasy Take: Glove-first prep catchers are not worth rostering, even in deep dynasty leagues. And that's coming from someone who notoriously overvalues catching prospects.

10. Sam Weatherly

OFP: 50 ETA: 2023
Born: 05/28/99 Age: 22 Bats: L Throws: L Height: 6'4" Weight: 205
Origin: Round 3, 2020 Draft (#81 overall)

The Report: A former two-way player out of cold-weather Michigan, it hasn't been long since Weatherly committed to pitching. Since that transition he has become demonstrably better, as his fastball/slider combo needed a ton of work on the control side. After previously walking more than a batter per inning, he took charge as the Friday night starter for Clemson this past spring and put up insane strikeout rates, to the tune of almost two per inning while cutting the walk rate by half. The 6-foot-4 frame offers a lot of arms and legs in the delivery, when he gets out of sync the command issues begin. When repeated, the fastball is TrackMan-friendly with carry up in the zone while sitting in the mid-90s. The real story is the slider, featuring a wipeout quality, oftentimes located better than his heater.

Development Track: He's shown just how good he can be when fully focusing on pitching. Ensuring he doesn't take a step back with the bases-on-balls will be necessary if he's to remain a starter long-term. Additionally, the changeup–which has mostly been a show-me pitch–will also need to come along at some point. Like any other college strikeout artist, you run him out there as a starter as long as possible knowing if things don't work out he can always rely on a dynamic 1-2 punch as a reliever.

Variance: High. In order for him to make it into the rotation he's going to need to clear two distinct hurdles (command and third pitch) that are far from gimmes. However, he does offer something as a valued relief pitcher in the event he stumbles.

J.P. Breen's Fantasy Take: Friends don't let friends draft potential relievers when they have yet to appear on a professional mound (outside of instructs).

The Prospects You Meet Outside The Top Ten

Solid pitching prospects, but limited upside

Karl Kauffmann   RHP   Born: 08/15/97   Age: 23   Bats: R   Throws: R   Height: 6'2"   Weight: 200   Origin: Round 2, 2019 Draft (#77 overall)

The staff ace of the 2019 College World Series runner-up rode his amateur success into being a Competitive Balance B pick that July. After throwing 114 innings that spring and summer, the Rockies shut him down in preparation for what was hoped to be a fast-moving pro trajectory in 2020. Since 2020 didn't happen, the Rockies added him to alternate site to get reps. The profile lacks upside as it doesn't feature a true out pitch, but instead relies on preventing hard contact and throwing strikes with an above-average fastball and slider.

Prospects to dream on a little

Warming Bernabel SS Born: 06/06/02 Age: 19 Bats: R Throws: R Height: 6'0" Weight: 180 Origin: International Free Agent, 2018
Signed for $900,000 out of the Dominican in 2018, Bernabel isn't selling jeans but also isn't selling out for the kind of bat speed and barrel control that can handle plus major league velocity. I don't know if he will be ready for a full-season ball assignment in 2021, but I'll be asking around the AZ complex about him.

MLB-ready arms, but probably relievers

Lucas Gilbreath LHP Born: 03/05/96 Age: 25 Bats: L Throws: L Height: 6'1" Weight: 185 Origin: Round 7, 2017 Draft (#206 overall)
Perhaps it's a little odd to see a 40-man add who was last seen posting a near-6 ERA in Advanced-A as a 23-year-old here, but when said 40-man add is a lefty popping 100 in short bursts, it becomes quite explicable. Gilbreath more likely settles in as a 95-and-a-slider guy, but he's a *lefty* 95-and-a-slider guy, and could be a useful bullpen arm in 2021. And if he can be a 100-and-a-slider guy, there's an argument for him in the 10 spot over Weatherly.

You were going to ask about him in the comments

Riley Pint RHP Born: 11/06/97 Age: 23 Bats: R Throws: R Height: 6'5" Weight: 225 Origin: Round 1, 2016 Draft (#4 overall)
Pint was not added to the 40-man, although he was hitting triple digits in instructs himself. In what is becoming an unfortunately familiar refrain for the former fourth-overall pick, reports varied, from upper-90s heat and a plus-plus flashing slider around the zone enough to make it work to 20 command/control of a low-90s fastball. And these reports came a week apart.

Top Talents 25 and Under (as of 4/1/2021):

1. Zac Veen, OF
2. Brendan Rodgers, SS/2B
3. Ryan Rolison, LHP
4. Ryan Vilade, SS/3B
5. Michael Toglia, OF
6. Chris McMahon, RHP
7. Aaron Schunk, 3B

8. Brenton Doyle, OF
9. Colton Welker, 3B
10. Drew Romo, C

We were already preliminarily dreading ranking Brendan Rodgers as a prospect again this offseason when he was removed from our immediate purview by the changes to the service time rules. But that just left him to my purview on the 25-and-under beat. Alas.

For a few years now, we've been concerned about Rodgers' approach against advanced pitching negatively impacting his hit tool. In very limited MLB time, that's borne out in a 4/33 BB/K ratio and poor all-around offensive performance. We're now also worried about what seem to be chronic shoulder injuries; after a season-ending surgery in 2019 for a torn labrum, he missed all of September 2020 with a capsule strain in the same shoulder. There's still a lot of underlying talent and skill here, but there's a lot of ifs now, too.

For the rest of the eligible non-prospects … well, it's kind of bleak. Peter Lambert made this list last year, just barely, and then blew out his elbow in summer camp and had Tommy John surgery in July. He missed all of 2020 and rates to miss much or all of 2021, too. Ryan Castellani took a regular turn in Colorado's rotation for much of the season. He put up a 7.92 DRA and walked more hitters than he struck out. The date cutoffs probably hurt more here than in most systems, with Germán Márquez and Antonio Senzatela both missing by fewer than three months.

Part 3: Featured Articles

Rockies All-Time Top 10 Players

by Steven Goldman

POSITION PLAYERS

TODD HELTON, 1B (1997-2013)
A career .316/.414/.539 hitter, and not all of it was the high-altitude environment—Helton hit .287/.386/.469 on the road. Consider that over the span of his career the average major league first baseman hit .275/.357/.470, and that not all of them were as good on the fielding job as he was. Chronic back problems rendered the second half of the nine-year contract extension he signed in 2001 (it was set to begin in 2003) an unfortunate slog, but that doesn't invalidate what came before. The team's first-round selection in the 1995 draft, the Toddfather was the only player available who provided a defensible reason for leaving Roy Halladay on the board, even with the benefit of hindsight. In the years since his retirement, the Rockies haven't come within light years of replacing him and seem almost happier not trying.

DJ LeMAHIEU, 2B (2012-2018)
Baseball is a confounding game sometimes; you can evaluate things correctly and still be wrong. In 2011 the Cubs looked at LeMahieu and saw… Well, not much. We probably weren't far off when we wrote, "LeMahieu has fine contact-hitting skills, but he struggled to do much beyond thwacking singles, keeping his ceiling low… lacks the power of a starting third baseman or the range of a middle infielder." The Cubs dealt him to Colorado with outfielder Tyler Colvin for former first-round flameout Ian Stewart. It took a few years, a bodybuilding intervention by Charlie Blackmon, and a retooled swing, but over a period of five years LeMahieu went from a low-power, low-OBP singles hitter to a more selective batter who looked for his pitch and when he got it had the ability to drive it. There was still every reason to believe that a good deal of his productivity

was Coors-driven but ask the Yankees what they think about that theory. They'll say the same thing Theo Epstein does when you ask about having traded LeMahieu. In both cases the answer won't be printable in a family book.

VINNY CASTILLA, 3B (1993-1999, 2004, 2006)

Ask even a casual fan to name a great pitcher born in Mexico and they'll likely be able to shout, "Fernando!" Slightly more knowledgeable fans might also reel off names like Teddy Higuera, Ismael Valdez, Joakim Soria, or even one of the pitchers listed just below, Jorge De La Rosa. Naming the best position players from Estados Unidos Mexicanos is more difficult because the list is—unfortunately—shorter. Top choices include 1954 AL batting champion Bobby Avila and the third baseman the Rockies selected with the 40th pick in the 1992 expansion draft. At the time, it seemed as if Castilla's high upside was that of a low-offense utility infielder. He was a career .255/.302/.392 hitter in the minors, which portends little more than a lot of bus rides in the bushes, assuming teams like your glove and your personality. He could pound a fastball, but he had little in the way of patience or power. The former never did arrive, but the latter sure did—from 1994 to 1995 he jumped from three home runs in 52 games to 32 in 139, then hit 126 over the next three seasons. While not all great Rockies players deserve to be tarred with the "product of Coors Field" epithet, Castilla demonstrably was one: He was a .333/.377/.604 hitter at home during his Rockies years, .254/.301/.452 everywhere else. That's not to say that being able to take advantage of one's environment isn't a skill; even granted a handicap, not every player can slug .600. Conversely, enough can that the road to salvation for the Rockies still lies in on-base percentage, the one thing Castilla was incapable of supplying.

NOLAN ARENADO, 3B (2013-2020)

Operating under the misapprehension that baseball teams are always building towards something, Arenado signed an eight-year contract extension with the Rockies in 2019. Then the scales fell from his eyes and the end came swiftly. The three-time National League home run leader and eight-time Gold Glover will be able to justify his place in the lineup with his glove even if he hits only at his career road rates of .264/.322/.471. The Rockies' inability to build around him won't be so easily rationalized.

TROY TULOWITZKI, SS (2006-2015)

He had Ripken-esque offensive skills without Ripken-esque durability and was gone too soon. Nevertheless, he got about two-thirds of the way to a Hall of Fame career, with a half-dozen seasons almost any shortstop in history would be proud to include on the back of his baseball card.

TREVOR STORY, SS (2016-Present)
Not bad for a first-round compensation pick earned due to the loss of Octavio Dotel after a Rockies career lasting all if eight games. When he first reached the majors he had what seemed like an unsustainable strikeout rate, one that would put an upper ceiling on his batting average. Beginning in year three he cut that rate just enough that he's hit .292 instead of the .253 of years one and two. His aggressive, fly-heavy approach will be tested when he inevitably departs this eternally rebuilding team—he's on the cusp of free agency—but much as with the exiled Arenado, his glove should keep him on the field even if he's no longer a threat to hit 35 home runs.

LARRY WALKER, OF (1995-2004)
"Baseball's meal on a bun," we said of Walker in 2003, "one of those guys worth the price of admission." Always frangible, the future Hall of Famer (hooray for being freed from the soft idiocy of counting stats) was nevertheless electric when he played. One of the few times Rockies management tried to answer the question, "What if we pay a really, really top-shelf ballplayer to come here?" resulted in 10 years of play from a fantastic all-around athlete still in his prime. Walker could hit, run, and field, was patient and powerful, and to the extent the environment rewarded his performance (he hit .384/.464/.715 at home, .285/.385/.514 on the road) it was enhancing his abilities, not creating an illusion of them. Coors Field helps all hitters to some extent, but if it helped them equally then Neifi Perez would have been Larry Walker, too, so the latter's exploitation of it reflects skill. You have to have real ability to receive all of its gifts.

MATT HOLLIDAY, OF (2004-2008, 2018)
Drafted out of high school in the seventh round of the 1998 draft, Holliday's six years climbing up the minor league ladder gave very little reason to believe that he'd play 1903 games in the big leagues and hit 316 home runs with a .299 average. In two full seasons at Double-A he hit .264/.343/.393 which is an argument for going to college, not the All-Star Game. Two years after reaching the majors, he took yet another leap forward, pushing his production to in-the-MVP-conversation levels. He came close to getting the award in 2007 when he won the NL batting title at .340 and also led in hits (216), doubles (50), total bases (386), and RBI (137). Most of the second half of his career was spent with the Cardinals, where he showed that all of that unexpected productivity wasn't solely a gift of the ballpark.

CARLOS GONZALEZ, OF (2009-2018)
The Rockies being the Rockies, they had to trade Holliday at 29. At least they got back a quality reliever in Huston Street and the potent GarGo. From 2009 through 2013 he hit .307/.368/.552 and played a Gold Glove left field. But there were injuries, so many injuries. He didn't necessarily have more stays on the disabled

list than the average player, but you know how, when someone says a player is "day to day" the kneejerk response is to reply, "Aren't we all?" It's true, but CarGo was the exception—he was more likely to be day to day than any man, woman, child, or wildebeest on the planet. Not only did he have the usual assortment of strains and contusions, he missed time with non-specific viruses, strep throat, the flu, an appendectomy, and "steak knife at home." The second five years of his Rockies stay was resultantly less fun, with .273/.331/.481 rates. There was even a 40-home season in there, but his defensive skills had eroded and the production, when you accounted for Coors Field, was average to subpar. The moral of the story: Don't use steak knives; have mom cut it for you.

CHARLIE BLACKMON, OF (2011-PRESENT)

He didn't get to play every day until he was 27, in part due to injuries, and he didn't blossom as a truly above-average player until he was 29. Much like Holliday before him, his early minor league results didn't portend a star. He was badly impatient, an approach he carried to the major leagues; he drew 14 walk in his first 151 games (over three seasons) and 31 in his first full season. To his credit, he was aware of this and worked to correct it. While he didn't turn into Ed Yost, he did see more pitches. That allowed him to stay away from pitches he couldn't drive and swing at those he could (as opposed to swinging at everything regardless). Coming up on 34, he's rapidly losing speed, the results of which are visible in his fielding metrics. We'll see if he has another reinvention left in the tank.

PITCHERS

STEVE REED, RHP (1993-1997, 2003-2004)

It says something about the Rockies' ongoing pitching problems that a submarining non-closer ranks as highly as he does in the organization's history. Signed by the Giants after not being drafted in 1988, left unprotected in the 1992 expansion draft, Reed never got much respect, but you don't get to pitch in the majors until you're 40 without being good. In 1995 he pitched 84 innings, 17.1 more than the team's closer, and recorded a 2.14 ERA as he held same-side hitters to a .196 average. Left-handers were more of a problem given his approach—in 2001 (post-Rockies) they hit .519/.629/.904 against him—but with proper usage he was as valuable as the pitchers who piled up the saves. As we wrote in 2005, "If you run into Steve on the street, salute him, buy him a beer, pummel those who refuse to genuflect in his presence. Whatever feels right."

PEDRO ASTACIO, RHP (1997-2001)

One of three Rockies to date to record 200 strikeouts in a season, Astacio was acquired from the Dodgers for Eric Young the Elder after failing to find consistency under Tommy Lasorda. His first full season with the Rockies was

6.23-ERA disaster, but he rebounded to post ERAs in the 5.00s, which sounds bad but given the park and league environment was actually above average. Unfathomably below average was his arrest on domestic violence charges in 2000 (he pleaded guilty to a lesser charge and was sentenced to probation). It was a time before Major League Baseball considered such crimes a subject for discipline and Astacio went on to get many more chances. His shoulder began to go around that time and those opportunities did not reward the teams that offered them.

JASON JENNINGS, RHP (2001-2006)
"They say you can't do it, but sometimes it doesn't always work," Casey Stengel said in 1954. Say that quietly to yourself when first-round draft-picks are talked about as sure things. Jennings, a product of Baylor University, where he was a two-way player, was Baseball America's 1999 College Player of the Year. He was tabbed by the Rockies with the 16th-overall pick of that year's draft. He featured a power sinker, an offering that would later work for other pitchers pitching in Denver. On August 23, 2001 he made his major league debut at Shea Stadium and accomplished something that even Babe Ruth had failed to do, pitching a complete-game shutout and hitting a home run along the way. There were other highs over the next five years, including the 2002 Rookie of the Year award. Jennings' 2006, in which he logged a 3.78 ERA in 212 innings, remains of the best in team history. It was one of only two seasons in which he overcame wandering command, and his arm failed soon thereafter.

AARON COOK, RHP (2002-2011)
Cook had the second-lowest strikeout rate of the current millennium, whiffing only 3.7 batters per nine innings. Even though he was extremely good at inducing ground balls, his let-'em-hit-it approach should have been disastrous in the wide Denver expanses. It wasn't. His ERA at home was 4.65, fourth-lowest in team history (300 innings minimum). He threw hard but learned to add and subtract velocity to induce weak contact. The Rockies rarely gave him the offensive or defensive support he needed to put together gaudy numbers but for 2008 when he went 16-9 with a 3.96 ERA. Thereafter he struggled with health and a rise in his walk rate that his high hit-rate couldn't withstand. The two trends converged to finish him by the time he was 33, though he's still the team's all-time leader in innings pitched.

UBALDO JIMENEZ, RHP (2006-2011)
The best pitcher in Rockies history, Jimenez had a fastball that sat in the mid-90s and had the rare ability to induce both strikeouts and an above-average number of grounders. It was the perfect approach for Coors Field—either make them hit it on the ground or don't let them hit it at all. Thus his ERA at home was 3.67, the best in team history by far. His only flaw was fluctuating command, the result of

imperfect mechanics. In 2011 he went on an incredible run to begin the season, going 11-1 with a 0.93 ERA in his first 12 starts, including a no-hitter against the Braves. It wasn't sustainable, of course, but he still finished 19-8 with a 2.88 ERA. He never reclaimed those heights and within half a season he was traded out of town.

JORGE DE LA ROSA, LHP (2008-2016)

Passed from the Diamondbacks to the Sultanes do Monterrey to the Red Sox to the Diamondbacks to the Brewers to the Royals to the Rockies by the time he was 27, De La Rosa donned the black and purple with a career record of 15-23, an ERA of 5.85 and an unsustainable 5.2 walks per nine innings. When he was with the Red Sox, Dan Duquette called him "The Mexican John Rocker," which probably really upset John Rocker. Though he was a hard-throwing lefty who would never be an innings eater (he peaked at 185 in 2009), it turned out De La Rosa was better suited to starting. After 2011 Tommy John surgery knocked his fastball down a peg he was able to vary his approach enough to maintain effectiveness for another three seasons. He's the franchise's all-time leader in wins and strikeouts.

JHOULYS CHACIN, RHP (2009-2014)

He came to the majors cut in the shape of Ubaldo with some of the same plusses and minuses—strikeouts, grounders, and wildness—but with a larger repertoire of pitches. He, De La Rosa, and Jimenez have been the only pitchers in team history to be able to pitch in the ballpark at anything like a consistently high level. Unfortunately, nature has designed pitchers such that for most pitchers it's strikeouts or grounders, but not both. When shoulder problems set in, the Rockies cut him with unseemly haste. He'd eventually pitch well again, but not for them.

JON GRAY, RHP (2015-PRESENT)

We can only speculate about the road not taken: Gray was drafted three times—by the Royals in the 13th round (2010), the Yankees in the 10th round (2011), and by the Rockies in the first round (2013), at which point he finally signed. That last earned him a sweet $4.8 million bonus, whereas 2011 10th-rounders received anywhere from $20,000 to $395,000. He gambled on himself and won enough money to set him up for life, and he's only added to that pot in the major leagues. Yet, if you will forgive a cliché, money can't buy you happiness or a sense of accomplishment. Gray has had a good career with the Rockies if an inconsistent one. As he crests the hill of his 29th birthday his velocity has dropped and his results have cratered, although outcomes from the truncated 2020 season are not to be trusted. Still, if Gray is indeed on the downside, he might wonder what the back of his baseball card would have looked like had he signed with one of those other teams, what else he might have won. Arenado was able to force his way out of town so that he'll have at least a partial answer to that question. Gray might not be so fortunate.

GERMAN MÁRQUEZ, RHP (2016-2020)
Signed by the Rays out of Valenzuela, traded to the Rockies with Jake McGee for Corey Dickerson and Kevin Padlo. You imagine they'd like to have that one back, although since Marquez is past his salary-controlled years they would have traded him by now. The club's all-time leader in strikeout-walk ratio is a hard thrower who (this may sound familiar by now) gets both strikeouts and grounders. Still only 26 and signed through 2023 with a team option for 2024, he's as good a bet as any to emerge as the team's all-time leader in career value by a pitcher.

KYLE FREELAND, LHP (2017-Present)
A Denver native, he was the eighth-overall pick of the 2014 and a good one. That's saying quite a lot given that Aaron Nola, Michael Conforto, Trea Turner, Matt Chapman, and Jack Flaherty were also taken in the first round. It's saying yet more to note he doesn't throw hard by today's standards. His fastball sits around 92 mph, one reason that fellow lefty Carlos Rodon was picked five spots ahead of him. His 2018 season was the best by any pitcher in team history, besting even Jimenez's 2011. That year he went 10-2 with a 2.40 ERA at home. He doesn't get many strikeouts relative to his peers but utilizes his cutter and change to induce weak contact. If he hasn't been able to replicate '18 thus far it's because there's always an excess element of luck playing a part in the success or failure of pitchers who let 'em hit it, especially with this team, this park, this city.

A Taxonomy of 2020 Abnormalities

by Rob Mains

I'm going to start this with a trivia question. Trust me, it's relevant. Don't bother skipping to the end of the article to find the answer, it's not there.

Only five players have appeared in 140 or more games for 16 straight seasons. Who are they?

It's a trivia question starting off an essay, so you know how this works: Whatever you guessed, you're wrong. It's okay. As someone who purchased this book, chances are good that you're an educated baseball fan. But the circumstances behind 2020 force us to abandon, or at least seriously question, some of our favorite patterns and crutches for evaluating the game we love.

We just completed what was undoubtedly the strangest season in MLB history. No fans, geographically limited schedule, universal DH, seven-inning twin bills, runners on second in extra innings, a 16-team postseason, a club playing at a Triple-A stadium. Some of these changes will likely persist (sorry), but we've never had so many tweaks dumped on us all at once, at least not since they figured out how many balls were in a walk.

And the biggest, of course, was the 60-game season. The 19th century was dotted with teams that went bankrupt before the season ended, but the lone season with only 60 scheduled games was 1877. That year there were only six teams, the league rostered a total of 77 players (just 16 more than the 2020 Marlins), and batters called for pitches to be thrown high or low by the pitcher, who was 50 feet away. We can say the 2020 season was easily the shortest ever for recognizable baseball.

As such, it'll stand out. Few abbreviated seasons do. Just about everybody reading this knows the 1994 season ended after Seattle's Randy Johnson struck out Oakland's Ernie Young for the last out of the Mariners-A's game on August 11. The ensuing player strike wiped out the rest of the season and the postseason. Teams played only 112-117 games that year.

And many of you know that a strike in the middle of the 1981 season split the season in two, resulting in the only Division Series until 1995. Teams played only 103-111 games that year, the shortest regular season since 1885.

Those two seasons are memorable. So when we see that nobody drove in 100 runs in 1981, or that Greg Maddux was the only pitcher with 180 or more innings pitched in 1994, we think, "Of course. Strike year."

But we don't remember other short years. You might not recall that the 1994 strike spilled into the next year, chopping 18 games off the 1995 schedule. You might've read that the 1918 season, played during the last pandemic, ended after Labor Day due to the government's World War I "work or fight" order. A strike erased the first week and a half of the 1972 season, but that year's best known as the last time pitchers batted in the American League.

The point is, while we don't remember small changes to the schedule, we remember the big ones. The 1981 mid-season strike. The 1994 season- and Series-ending strike. And, of course, the pandemic-shortened 2020 season. We won't need a reminder why Marcell Ozuna's 18 homers were the fewest to lead the National League in a century. (Literally; Cy Williams led with 15 in 1920.)

Now, about that trivia question. The five players are Hank Aaron, Brooks Robinson, Pete Rose, Ichiro Suzuki, and Johnny Damon. The one nobody gets, of course, is Damon, and a lot of people miss Ichiro, whose last season of 140-plus games came garbed in the red-orange and ocean blue of Miami when he was 42. That's half of what makes it a good question. The other half is the two guys whom many think made the list but didn't. Lou Gehrig? His streak started in the Yankees' 42nd game of the 1925 season and lasted only 13 seasons after that. And everybody assumes Cal Ripken Jr. did it, having played 2,632 straight games over 17 seasons. But one of those 17 seasons was 1994, when the Orioles played only 112 games.

My point? *I just told you* everybody remembers the 1994 strike year, but everybody forgets it fell in the middle of Ripken's streak, separating the first twelve years from the last four. Just because we recall something doesn't mean it's always at the front of our minds.

Nobody is going to forget 2020, and baseball is obviously not the main reason. But there will come a time in the future when you're looking at a player's or a team's record, and there will be baffling numbers there for 2020, and you'll think, "I wonder what happened." (Not to mention the missing line for minor league players.) Just like you forgot that the 1994 strike limited Ripken to 112 games.

Try not to forget it, though. The 2020 season resulted in weird statistical results for several reasons.

There were only 60 games.

I know, duh. But that had impacts beyond counting stats like Ozuna's home run total or Yu Darvish and Shane Bieber leading the majors with eight wins. (I know, pitcher wins, but still.)

The 162-game season is the longest among major North American sports, and that duration gives us a gift. Over the course of a long season, small variations tend to even out. A player who has a ten-game hot streak will probably have a ten-game cold streak. A team that starts the year losing a bunch of close games will probably win a bunch of them. We get regression to the mean. Statistics stabilize.

Consider flipping a coin. Over the long run, we expect it to come up heads about half the time. But the fewer flips, the more variation there'll be. If you flip a coin six times, probability theory tells us you'll get at least two-third heads about 34 percent of the time. Flip it 30 times, your chance of two-thirds heads drops to five percent.

Or, relevant to this case, if you flip a coin 60 times, your chance of getting at least 36 heads—that's 60 percent—is 7.75 percent. Expand the coin-flipping to 162 times, and the chance of getting 60 percent heads drops to 0.73 percent.

In other words, the odds of an outcome that's 20 percent better (or worse) than expected is *more than ten times higher* when you flip your coin 60 times than when you do it 162 times. Call it small sample size, call lack of mean reversion, or call it luck not evening out, 162 is a lot more predictive than 60. You get much more variation over 60 games than over 162. Bieber's 1.63 ERA and 0.87 FIP aren't something we'd see over a full season, and neither is Javier Baéz's .203/.238/.360.

Some players' lines in 2020 look normal. Brian Anderson had an .811 OPS in 2019 and an .810 OPS in 2020. (He probably would have gotten that last point if he'd been given enough time.) But there are many like Bieber and Baéz, some of them from young players still establishing their talent levels. The answer to the question, "What went right or wrong for that guy in 2020?" is most likely "Nothing, it was just a 2020 thing."

Preseason training was abbreviated for hitters.

Every year, spring training drags. Players get tired of it, fans get tired of it, and you sure can tell sportswriters get tired of it. Yes, something to get everyone into shape is necessary, but does it really have to drag on for over a month? Can't we shorten it?

The 2020 season answered in the negative, at least for hitters. Warren Spahn is credited with saying that hitting is timing and pitching is upsetting timing. It appears nobody had his timing down after the abbreviated July summer camp. Through August 9—18 games into the season—MLB batters were hitting .230/.311/.395 with a .275 BABIP. That BABIP, had it held, would have been the lowest since 1968, the Year of the Pitcher. In recent years it's hovered around .300.

It didn't hold. Play returned to more normal levels the rest of the year: .249/.325/.425 with a .297 BABIP starting August 10. But batters whose play concentrated in those first two weeks wound up with ugly lines. Andrew

Benintendi went on the injured list with a season-ending rib cage strain on August 11. His final line: .103/.314/.128 in 14 games. Franchy Cordero went on the IL with a hamate bone fracture on August 9 and a .154/.185/.231 line. Even though he came back strong in a late September return, it was too late to repair his full-season numbers.

Preseason training was abbreviated for pitchers.
Every year, spring training drags. Players get tired of it, fans get tired of it ... wait, I already said that. But the abbreviated preseason was tough on pitchers, too. As noted, they had the upper hand coming out of the gate. But then they lost that hand. And then their arms, too.

The 2020 season was spread over 67 days. During those 67 days, 237 pitchers hit the Injured List, compared to 135 in the first 67 days of 2019. A lot of those IL stints, though, were COVID-19-related. Still, over the first 67 days of the 2019 season, there were 72 pitchers on the IL with arm injuries. That figure jumped to 110 in 2020, a 53 percent increase.

There are a number of factors contributing to pitcher arm injuries, ranging from usage to velocity, but it appears that attenuated preseason training played a role. A lot of pitchers had super-short seasons due to arm woes. Corey Kluber, Roberto Osuna, and Shohei Ohtani combined for seven innings, none after August 8. All suffered arm injuries. We'll never know whether they'd have fared better with a longer preseason, but we can guess how they probably feel.

Everybody played.
Rosters were set to expand from 25 to 26 in 2020, so even if we'd had a normal season, we'd have likely seen 2019's record of 1,410 players on MLB rosters broken. But due to the pandemic, rosters started the year at 30 and were cut to only 28. Add multiple COVID-19 absences and the revolving door caused by poor starts by hitters and a rash of pitcher arm injuries, and 1,289 players appeared in MLB games in 2020. The comparable figure over the first 67 days of the 2019 season was 1,109. That 16 percent increase works out to an average of six more players per team in 2020 compared to a similar slice of 2019. A future look back at 2020 rosters will include a lot of unfamiliar names.

Plus became a minus.
In advanced metrics, we adjust batter and pitcher performance for park and league/era variations. A plus sign appended to the end of a measure means that it's adjusted for park and league. It's scaled to an average of 100, with higher figures above average and lower figures below average. (Similarly, a metric with a minus is also park- and league-adjusted and scaled to 100, with lower values better.) Here at BP, our advanced measure of offensive performance is DRC+. Baseball-Reference has OPS+ and FanGraphs has wRC+.

Using park and league adjustments, we can compare Dante Bichette's 1995 Steroid Era season at pre-humidor Coors Field (.340/.364/.620, 40 homers, 128 RBI, MVP runner-up) with Jim Wynn's 1968 Year of the Pitcher season at the cavernous Astrodome (.269/.376/.474, 26 homers, 67 RBI, no MVP votes). It's not close. DRC+, OPS+, and wRC+ all give the nod to Wynn, handily. This is a useful tool. As my Baseball Prospectus colleague Patrick Dubuque tweeted last fall, "Please note that when I ask how you are, I am already adjusting for era."

The 2020 season messes up plus (and minus) stats for two reasons. First, the park adjustment was based on only 30 home games instead of the usual 81. Everything noted above regarding the short season applies, literally doubly, to park effect calculations. DRC+ uses a single-season park factor. OPS+ uses a three-year average and wRC+ five years. The figure for 2020 is suspect.

Second, OPS+ and wRC+ adjust for league: American and National. (DRC+ adjusts for opponent, regardless of league.) While there were two leagues in 2020, they were an artificial construct. To reduce travel, teams played opponents geographically, not based on league. There weren't two leagues, American and National. There were three, Western, Central, and Eastern.

That makes a difference because teams in the same league played in different run-scoring environments. AL teams scored 4.58 runs per game, NL teams 4.71. That's a small difference. But teams in the East scored 0.21 more runs per game (4.95) than teams in the West (4.74), and they both scored a lot more than Central teams (4.25). Adjusting for league misses that difference, so this book will be safe in that regard, but other sources may be distorted somewhat.

Not every game was a "game."
In 2020, the rising tide of strikeouts was finally stemmed. Strikeouts per team per game fell from 8.8 in 2019 to 8.7 in 2020. That marked the first decline after 14 straight annual increases.

In 2020, the rising tide of strikeouts rose higher. Batters struck out in 23.4 percent of plate appearances compared to 23.0 percent in 2019. That marked the 15th straight annual increase.

Both are true statements.

Because of two rule changes—seven-inning doubleheaders and runners on second in extra innings—games in 2020 were unprecedented in their brevity. There were 37.0 plate appearances per game in 2020. The only years with fewer were 1904 and 1906-1909. The average game in 2020 entailed 8.61 innings pitched, the fewest since 1899.

So when you see any per-game stats for 2020, you need to increase them by 3 or 4 percent to get them on equal footing with recent years.

Colorado Rockies 2021

Or, better, just ignore them. Last year happened. There were major league games contested between major league teams. But when you're looking at those physical or electronic baseball cards, when you're weaving narratives over why this young player's inevitable rise to stardom fell apart or why that old veteran rekindled his magic, don't linger on the 2020 line. It was just too weird.

Thanks to Lucas Apostoleris for research assistance.

—*Rob Mains is an author of Baseball Prospectus.*

Tranches of WAR

by Russell A. Carleton

We ask "replacement level" to be a lot of things. Sometimes contradictory things. Sometimes I wonder if we know what it even means anymore. The original idea was that it represented the level of production that a team could expect to get from "freely available talent", including bench players, minor leaguers, and waiver wire pickups. It created a common benchmark to compare everyone to, and for that reason, it represented an advancement well beyond what was available at the time. In fact, it created a language and a framework for evaluating players that was not just better but *entirely* different than what came before it.

But then we started mumbling in that language. The idea behind "wins above replacement" was one part sci-fi episode and one part mathematical exercise. Imagine that a player had disappeared before the season and suddenly, in an alternate timeline, his team would have had to replace him. The distance between him and that replacement line was his value. We need to talk about that alternate timeline.

Without getting too into 2:00 am "deep conversations" with extensive navel-gazing, it's worth thinking about why one player might not be playing, while another might.

- A player might not be playing because he has a short-term injury or his manager believes that he needs a day off.
- A player might not be playing because he has a longer-term injury that requires him to be on the injured list.

There's a difference here between these two situations. In particular, the first one generally *doesn't* involve a compensatory roster move, while the second one does. It's possible, though not guaranteed, that the person who will be replacing the injured/resting player would be the same in either case. That matters. Teams generally carry a spare part for all eight position players on the diamond, although in the era of a four-player bench, those spare parts usually are the backup plan for more than one spot.

Colorado Rockies 2021

A couple of years ago, I posed a hypothetical question. Suppose that a team had two players in its system fighting for a fourth outfielder spot. One of them was a league average hitter, but would be worth 20 runs below average if allowed to play center field for a full season. One of them was a perfectly average fielder, but would be 15 runs below average as a hitter, if allowed to play an entire season. Which of the two should the team roster? It's tempting to say the second one, as overall, he is the better player. That misses the point. A league average hitter on the bench isn't just a potential replacement for an injured outfielder. He might also pinch hit for the light-hitting shortstop in a key spot. You keep the average hitter on the roster, even though he isn't a hand-in-glove fit for one specific place on the field, because being a bench player is a different job description than being a long-term fill-in for someone. If you find yourself in need of a longer-term fill-in, you can bring the other guy up from AAA.

When we're determining the value of an everyday player though, if he had disappeared before the season and a team would have had to replace his production, they likely would have done it with a player who was a long-term fill-in type because they would have had to replace a guy who played everyday. Maybe that's the same guy that they would have rostered on their bench anyway, but we don't know. It gets to the query of what we hope to accomplish with WAR. Are we looking for an accurate modeling of reality or are we looking for a common baseline to compare everyone to? Both have their uses, but they are somewhat different questions.

Let's talk about another dichotomy.

- A player might not be playing because he isn't very good and is a bench-level player.
- A player might not be playing because there is another player on the team who has a situational advantage that makes him the better choice today. The classic case of this is a handedness platoon. On another day, he might be a better choice.

When we think about player usage, I think we're still stuck in the model that there are starters and there are scrubs. We have plenty of words for bench players or reserves or backups or utility guys. We do still have the word "platoon" in our collective vocabulary, but in the age of short benches, it's hard to construct one. It's always been hard to construct them. You have to find two players who hit with different hands, have skill sets that complement each other, and probably play the same position. In the era of the short bench, one of them had probably better double as a utility player in some way. Baseball has a two-tiered language geared toward the idea of regulars and reserves. The fact that it was so easy for me to find plenty of synonyms for "a player whose primary function is to come into a game to replace a regular player if he is injured or resting" should tell you something.

I'm always one to look for "unspoken words" in baseball. What is it called when someone is both half of a platoon and the utility infielder? That guy exists sometimes, but he reveals himself in that role—usually by accident. We don't have a word for that, and whenever I find myself saying "we don't have a word for that", I look for new opportunities. What do you call it, further, when the job of being the utility infielder is decentralized across the whole infield with occasional contributions from the left fielder? It's not even a "super-utility" player. What happens when you build your entire roster around the idea that everyone will be expected to be a triple major?

⚾ ⚾ ⚾

I think someone else beat me to this one, and on a grand scale. Platoons work because we know that hitters of the opposite hand to the pitcher get better results than hitters of the same hand, usually to the tune of about 20 points of OBP. If you want to express that in runs, it usually comes out to somewhere around 10 to 12 runs of linear weights value prorated across 650 PA. But hang on a second, now let's say that we have two players who might start today, both of roughly equal merit with the bat. One has a handedness advantage, but is the worse fielder of the two. In that case, as long as his "over the course of a season" projection as a fielder at whatever position you want to slot him into is less than a 10-run drop from the guy he might replace, then he's a better option today.

We're not used to thinking of utility players as bat-first options, who would play below-average defense at three different infield positions. That guy might hook on as a 2B/3B/LF type (Howie Kendrick, come on down!) but teams usually think to themselves that they need as their utility infielder someone who "can handle" shortstop, the toughest of the infield spots to play. If someone can do that *and* hit well, he's probably already starting somewhere, so he's not available as a utility infielder. It's easier for those glove guys to find a job. In a world where the replacement for a shortstop *has to be* the designated utility infielder, that makes sense.

But as we talked about last week, we're living in a different world. The rate at which a replacement for a regular starter turns out to be *another starter* shifting over to cover has gone way up over the last five years. There was always some of it in the game, but this has been a supernova of switcheroos. Now if your second baseman is capable of playing a decent shortstop, that 2B/3B/LF guy can swap in. He's not actually playing shortstop, and maybe the defense suffers from the switch, but if he's got enough of a bat, he might outhit those extra fielding miscues. And in doing so, he is effectively your backup shortstop.

Somewhere along the lines, teams got hip to the idea of multi-positional play from their regulars. I've written before about how you can't just put a player, however athletic, into a new position and expect much at first. The data tell us that. Eventually, players can learn to be multi-positionalists, but it takes time, roughly on the order of two months, before they're OK. But there's a hidden message in there. If you give a player some reps at a new spot, he's a reasonably gifted athlete and somewhat smart and willing to learn, he could probably pick it up enough to get to "good enough," and it doesn't take forever. You just have to be purposeful about it. Maybe you get to the point where you can start to say "he's still below average but we could move him there and get another bat into the lineup, and it's a net win."

Teams have started to build those extra lessons into their player development program. It used to be seen as a mark of weakness to be relegated to "utility player" because that meant that you were a bench player (all those synonyms above come with a side of stigma). Now, it's a way of building a team. If you get a few reps in the minors (where it doesn't count) at a spot, you'll have at least played the spot at game speed before. There are limits to how far you can push that. A slow-footed "he's out in left field because we don't have the DH" guy is never going to play short, but maybe your third baseman can try second base and not look like a total moose out there.

⚾ ⚾ ⚾

Back to WAR. I'd argue that the world of starters and scrubs is slowly disintegrating, for good cause. In the event that a regular starter really does go down with an injury–ostensibly, the alternate universe scenario that WAR is attempting to model–it makes the team a little more resilient to replacing him. And the good news is that you're more likely to be able to replace him with the best of the bench bunch, rather than the third-best guy, because the best guy doesn't have to be an exact positional match for the guy who got hurt. And that's what the manager would want to do. He'd want to replace that long-term production, not with an amalgam of everyone else who played that position, but with the best guy available from his reserves.

Now this is still WAR. We still want to retain the principle that we should be measuring a player, and not his teammates. We need some sort of common baseline, and despite what I just said, we'll still need some sort of amalgam. To construct that, I give to you the idea of the tranche. The word, if you've not heard it before, refers to a piece of a whole that is somehow segmented off. It's often used in finance to talk about layers of a financial instrument.

Here, I want you to consider that there are 30 starters at each of the seven non-battery positions (catchers should have their own WAR, since only a catcher can replace a catcher). We can identify them by playing time, and we can futz around with the definition a little bit if we need to. Next, among those who aren't in that starting pool, we identify the top tranche of the 30 best bench players, which I would again identify by playing time, and then the second and third and fourth and so on. If a player were to disappear, his manager would probably want to take a guy from that top tranche of the bench to replace him. In a world where even the starters can slide around the field, that becomes more feasible.

We can take a look at that top tranche and say "How many of them showed that they are able to play (first, second, etc.)?" and therefore could have directly substituted for the starter? How many of them could have been a direct substitute for our injured player? We don't know whether one of them would be on *a specific* team, but we can say that 40 percent of the time, a manager would have been able to draw from tranche 1 in filling the role, and 35 percent from tranche 2. But on tranche 1, we can also look at how many of those players played a position that could have then shifted and covered for that spot. We'd need some eligibility criteria for all of this (probably a minimum number of games played) but it would just be a matter of multiplication. Shortstop would be harder to fill, and managers would probably be dipping a little further down in the talent pool, and so replacement level would be lower, as it is now.

Doing some quick analysis, I found that the difference in just batting linear weights (haven't even gotten into running or fielding) between tranche 1 and tranche 2 in 2019 was about 6.5 runs, prorated across 650 PA. Between tranche 1 and tranche 3, it's 10.8 runs. The ability to shift those plate appearances up the ladder has some real value.

This part is important. We can also give credit to starters for the positions that they showed an ability to play, even if they didn't play them (this is the guy fully capable of playing center, but who's in a corner because the team already has a good center fielder) because he allows a team to carry a player who hits like a left fielder to functionally be the team's backup center fielder. He facilitates that movement upward among the tranches. We can start to appreciate the difference between a left fielder who would never be able to hack it in center (and the compensatory move that his team would have to make) and the left fielder who could do it, but just didn't have to very often.

Past that, you can continue to use whatever hitting and fielding and running metrics you like to determine a player's value, but when we get down to constructing that baseline, I'd argue we need a better conceptual and mathematical framework. It's going to require some more #GoryMath than we're used to, but I'd argue it's a better conceptualization of the way that MLB actually plays the game in 2020. If…y'know…MLB plays in 2020. If WAR is going to be our flagship statistic among the *acronymati*, then we need to acknowledge that it contains some old and starting-to-be-out-of-date assumptions about the game. We may need to tinker with it. Here's my idea for how.

—*Russell A. Carleton is an author of Baseball Prospectus.*

Secondhand Sport

by Patrick Dubuque

Back before time stopped, I liked to go to thrift stores. Now that I'm older, I rarely ever buy anything—I don't need much in my life, now—but I still enjoy the old familiar circuit: check to see if there are baseball cards to write about, look for board or card games to play with the kids, scan for random ironic jerseys, hit the book section. It takes ten, maybe fifteen minutes. Thrift stores are the antithesis of modern online shopping, because you don't know what they have, and you don't even really know what you want. It's junk, literal junk, stuff other people thought was worthless. That's what makes it great.

In an idealized economy, thrift stores shouldn't exist. Everybody has a living wage, and every product has a durability that exactly matches its desired life; nothing should need to be given away, no one should need to be given to. But then, thrift stores shouldn't work on a customer experience level, either. You wouldn't think an ethos of "let's make everything disorganized and hard to find" would lead to customer satisfaction, but low-budget retailers like TJ Maxx and Ross thrive on this model. People like bargain hunting as much for the hunting as the bargain; it's part of the experience, spending time as if it's a wager. There's a thrill, occasionally, in inefficiency.

In sports, the modern overuse of the word "inefficiency" is a condemnation: It insinuates that there is *an* efficiency, a correct way to be found, and that all other ways are wrong ways. It's prevalent in baseball but hardly contained to it; the lifehack, the Silicon Valley disruption are other examples of productivity creep in our daily lives. Their modern success makes plenty of sense. Maximization of resources, after all, is its own puzzle, and an industry of European board games is founded upon it. It's fun to take a system and optimize it, unravel it like a sudoku puzzle. If there's only one kind of genius, after all, there's no way anyone can fail to appreciate it.

Baseball has been hacking away at these perceived inefficiencies since its inception: platoons, bullpens, farm systems were all installed to extract more out of the tools at hand. But it's been a particular badge of the sabermetric movement, from Ken Phelps and his All-Star Team to Ricardo Rincon and the darlings of *Moneyball*. It's business, but it's also an ethos: the idea that there's treasure among the trash, something we all failed to appreciate until someone brought it to light.

It's the myth that made Sidd Finch so enticing, that fuels so many "best shape" narratives and new pitch promises. We all, athletes and unathletic sportswriters, want to believe that there's genius trapped inside us, and that it's just a matter of puzzling out the combination to unlock it. That our art, our style is the next inefficiency, waiting for our own Billy Beane. It's why we root for underdogs, and why we're excited for the Mike Tauchmans and the Eurubiel Durazos, champions of skin-deep mediocrity.

Except we aren't anymore, really. The days of "Free X" have descended beyond the ring of irony and into obscurity. There are still Xs to be freed, or at least one X, duplicated endlessly: Mike Ford, Luke Voit, Max Muncy. The undervalued one-dimensional slugger demonstrated how the game hasn't quite culturally caught up to its logical extreme. But for those who don't fit the rather spacious mold, times are grimmer. As Rob Arthur revealed several months ago, there's been a marked increase in the number of sub-replacement relievers. It's the outcome of a greater number of teams forced to play out games without the talent to win them, but it's also emblematic of the modern tendency of teams to dispose of their disposable assets, burning through cost-controlled arms the way that man chopped down forests in *The Lorax*. Stuff just isn't built to outlive their original owners anymore.

It's unsurprising, given how well-mined the market for inefficiencies has been of late. The disciples of the early analytics departments, and the disciples of those, have proliferated the league, with only a few backwater holdouts. The league has grown smarter, but every team has learned the same lesson. In fact, the phenomenon creates a peculiar kind of feedback loop: As teams value a specific subset of players or skills, prospective athletes learn to increase their own marketability by conforming themselves to the demands of their prospective employers.

And that's tragic, in the way that the extinction of animals is tragic; a certain amount of biodiversity in baseball has been lost. Shortstops hit like outfielders. Pitchers don't hit at all. Only the catchers remain idiosyncratic, thanks to the defensive demands of their position; eventually they too will be required to produce like everyone else, or they'll meet the fate of their battery mates. A perfect economy requires perfect production.

I mentioned earlier that more and more, I leave thrift stores empty-handed. It is true that I am more discerning than in the past; my bookshelves are full, and there are more streaming films than I will ever be able to watch. But there are other factors at play.

Thrift stores are, in a way, the bond markets of retail. When the economy is rough and other retailers are struggling, more people look secondhand for their products. But as recently as last year, publications were noting a reversal of the trend: Companies like Goodwill and Savers were expanding despite a strong economy. Publications credited a heightened sense of environmentalism and a rejection of cutting-edge fashion as drivers behind the increase, though the more likely answer is the modern American economy hasn't showered its favors equally, particularly among the young.

But it is more than just the economy. Baseball and thrift stores share something else in common, evident in our current conversations about re-starting the sport: They live in the gray area between public service and private enterprise. Thrift stores provide affordable necessities to lower-class citizens, and collectibles and fashion for the middle-class. Because of the success of the latter, prices have gone up across the board. Especially in terms of clothing, the middle-class flight from fashion into vintage has instead carried the aftereffects of fashion, including its costs, into a territory where people just want clothes. But there's another factor in the rise of prices, in the form of the internet.

The Goodwills of the world have grown smarter, too, employing the internet to extract full value from their detritus. Ebay, similarly, has lost much of the charm it had as a new frontier around the turn of the century. Everything has a price point now; even individual taste is no match for the algorithm, because anything rare, no matter how niche its market, is a collectible to someone.

The internet has had the same effect on thrift stores that sabermetrics has had on baseball; its equivalent to OBP was the bar scanner. As detailed in Slate, the rise of second-party stores on eBay and Amazon birthed an entire industry of used-good salespeople, armed with PDAs and scanners, buying books for three dollars to sell online for five. The author, Michael Savitz, reports earning $60,000 by working nearly 80 hours a week; he makes it clear that this is not a vocation of his choosing. It's long hours, with no real creativity or individuality, skimming the cream off of a local establishment and flipping it to someone with a little more money on the other side of the country. And once the vocation exists, the obvious question arises: why wait to put the wares out on the shelves? Why allow value to exist at all?

Nothing is ruined. Thrift stores will continue to sell polo shirts and DVDs, and baseball will continue to exist and make or lose money, depending on who you believe. But as we continue to refine our knowledge, we lose something in the conquest for efficiency, a delight born out of the unknown. The problem isn't the efficiency itself; we can't blame the booksellers, or the people sweeping freeways to collect grams of platinum from damaged catalytic converters. The problem is a system that requires this sort of profit-skimming behavior in order to feed families (or, for corporations, maximize shareholder return).

Colorado Rockies 2021

In times like these, with the 2020 season on the brink and the collective bargaining agreement close behind, it can often feel like the current situation is untenable. It can't keep going like this, even if we don't know what to do about it. But as with thrift stores, there's an equally irresistible feeling that it *has* to keep going, that it would be unimaginable to not have this broken, amazing sport. Both industries exist on an invisible foundation of friction, of chaos and unpredictability, even as both see their foundations buffed down to a perfect, untouchable polish. But if COVID-19 and its financial ramifications do, as some have suggested, make it such that the baseball that returns is fundamentally different than the baseball that came before, perhaps this is the time to lean in, and change the game even more. Fix bunting. Make defense more difficult. Create viable, alternate strategies. Add some chaos back into baseball. It's fun when no one knows quite where things are.

—*Patrick Dubuque is an author of Baseball Prospectus.*

Steve Dalkowski Dreaming

by Steven Goldman

We dream of being a pitcher, of starring in the major leagues. Depending on your age and your sense of historical perspective, you might imagine yourself as Walter Johnson, throwing harder than anyone else—hitting more batters than anyone else, too, but always feeling bad about it. You could picture yourself as a Tom Seaver or a David Cone, with all the stuff in the world but still being cerebral about it, thinking about so much more than burning 'em in there. There are so many models one could choose: You could be a Lefty Gomez, Jim Bouton, or Bill Lee, skilled, but not taking the whole thing too seriously, or a Lefty Grove, Bob Gibson, or Steve Carlton, powerful but treating each start like a mission to be survived instead of a game to be enjoyed.

Very few would dream of being Steve Dalkowski, the former Baltimore Orioles prospect who died of COVID-19 last week at the age of 80. Yet, there is something just as noble in Dalkowski's negative accomplishments—and accomplishments is what they are—as there is in the precision-engineered pitching of a Greg Maddux. You have to be very good to be that bad. Dalkowski had all of the stuff of the greatest pitchers but none of the command; his story is not one of failing to conquer his limitations, but striving against one of the cruelest hands that fate or genetics or personality can deal us: A desire to achieve great things which is almost but not quite matched by the ability to meet that goal.

As with Johnson, Grove, Bob Feller, and the rest of the hard-throwing pitchers who played before the advent of modern radar guns, we have to take the word of the players and coaches who saw Dalkowski pitch as to his velocity. He was a hard-drinking, maximum-effort pitcher who, if their memories are to be believed, consistently threw over 100 miles per hour. His was the Maltese Fastball, the stuff that dreams are made of. The problem is that velocity without command and control is still a good distance from utility. Dalkowski was the most effective towel you could design for a fish, the sleekest bathing suit intended to be worn by an astronaut, but that doesn't mean he wasn't beautiful: We can appreciate a journey even if it doesn't end at the intended destination.

Whether because of sloppy mechanics he couldn't calm, an inability to understand that a consistent 98 in the strike zone would likely be more effective than a consistent 110 out of it, or all that beer, Dalkowski could never make the adjustments that pitchers like Feller and Nolan Ryan made before him, possibly because he had so far to go: Feller, who never pitched in the minors, came up at 17 and spent three years walking almost seven batters per nine innings before settling in at 3.8 beginning when he was 20. Ryan started out walking over six batters per nine but gradually improved as his long career played out; for him to go from 6.2 walks per nine with the 1966 Greenville Mets to 3.7 with the 1989 Texas Rangers represents a 40 percent reduction. An equivalent improvement by Dalkowski would still have left him walking over 11 batters per nine innings.

Dalkowski was like *The Room* of pitchers, a player so bad he became good again. Cal Ripken, Sr., who both played with and managed Dalkowski, recalled in a 1979 *Sporting News* "where are they now" piece the occasion when the pitcher crossed up his catcher and his fastball, "hit the plate umpire smack in the mask. The mask broke all to pieces and the umpire wound up in the hospital for three days with a concussion. If they ever had a radar gun in those days, I'll bet Dalkowski would have been timed at 110 miles an hour."

Signed by the Orioles out of New Britain High in Connecticut in 1957, Dalkowski was sent to Kingsport in the Appalachian League, where he pitched 62 innings. He allowed only 22 hits in 62 innings, or 3.2 per nine, a number with no equivalent in major league history (though Aroldis Chapman came close in 2014), and also struck out 121 (17.6 per nine) and walked 129 (18.7). He was also charged with 39 wild pitches. That June, one of his fastballs clipped a Dodgers prospect named Bob Beavers and carried away part of his ear. "The first pitch was over the backstop, the second pitch was called a strike, I didn't think it was," Beavers said last year. "The third pitch hit me and knocked me out, so I don't remember much after that. I couldn't get in the sun for a while, and I never did play baseball again." Former minor leaguer Ron Shelton based the *Bull Durham* pitcher Nuke LaLoosh on Dalkowski. And yet, to see him as a figure of fun, an amusing loser, is to misunderstand something unique and strange.

Dalkowski kept on posting some of the strangest lines in baseball history. Pitching for the Stockton Ports of the Class C California League in 1960, he struck out 262 and walked 262 in 170 innings. Yet, he did improve, especially after pitching for Earl Weaver at Elmira in 1962. Weaver had previously had Dalkowski at Aberdeen in 1959, but wasn't ready to grapple with him then. This time he was. "I had grown more and more concerned about players with great physical abilities who could not learn to correct certain basic deficiencies no matter how much you instructed or drilled them," he related in his autobiography, *It's What You Learn After You Know It All That Counts*. He got permission from the Orioles to give all of his players the Stanford-Binet IQ test. "Dalkowski finished in the 1 percentile in his ability to understand facts. Steve, it was said to say, had the ability to do everything but learn." [sic]

IQ tests are problematic diagnostic tools, so take Weaver's estimate of Dalkowski's mental capabilities with a grain of salt. What's important is that even if he got to the right answer by way of the wrong reason, Weaver had learned something valuable. His insight was to stop asking Dalkowski to learn new pitches and just let him get by with the two that he had. Were Dalkowski a prospect today, that would have been a no-brainer: Can't develop a third pitch? The bullpen is right over there, sir. Player development wasn't like that then, but Weaver, temporarily Dalkowski's mentor, could let him work with what he had. According to Weaver, the pitcher responded: "In the final 57 innings he pitched that season Dalkowski gave up 1 earned run, struck out 110 batters, and walked only 11." It's not true—as per the *Elmira Star-Gazette*, as of late July, Dalkowski had walked 71 in 106 innings and finished with 114 in 160 innings, which means Dalkowski's control actually faded at the end of the season rather than improved—but that doesn't mean it didn't happen in some sense, just that it didn't happen that way. Again, it's the journey, not the destination, and his ERA was 3.04 so *something* had gone right.

Also along the way: The next spring, Orioles manager Billy Hitchcock was rooting for Dalkowski to make the team as a long-man—maybe Weaver had gotten through to him. There were things out of Weaver's control, like the universe's twisted sense of humor: that March, Dalkowski's elbow went "twang."

You sometimes read that it was the Orioles' insistence on Dalkowski learning the curve that did him in, but even if they hadn't learned their lesson, the injury was probably just a coincidence: Dalkowski had thrown an incredible number of pitches over the previous few years. Still, it testifies to the dangers of trying to get what you want and risking the loss of what you had. Dalkowski tried to come back, but the 110-mph stuff was gone. A pitcher with no control and no stuff is…a civilian. What followed were years of vagabond living, arrests for drunkenness. There were Alcoholics Anonymous meetings, assistance from baseball alumni associations, but none of it took. From the 1990s until the time of his passing he dwelt in an assisted living facility, suffering from alcohol-related dementia. He'd been a heavy drinker since his teenage years. As with all those pitches per game, there was a price to be paid. You make choices on the journey and some of them are irrevocable. It's like a fairy tale: "Bite of poison apple? Don't mind if I do."

In the aforementioned *Sporting News* profile, Chuck Stevens, the head of the Association of Professional Ballplayers of America, a ballplayer charity, said, "I've got nothing against drinking. I do it myself sometimes. But, I don't condone common drunkenness. We went through lots of heartache and many dollars, but Dalkowski didn't want to help himself and we weren't going to keep him drunk." The journey is *un*like a fairy tale: No one will come along and kiss it better, not if they're busy forming judgments.

In the end, we are left with a sort of philosophical chicken/egg conundrum: Is failing to meet your goals evidence of unfulfilled potential or the lack of it? Isn't what you did by definition what you were capable of doing? Or could you have broken through to something better with the right help, the right lucky break? These are unanswerable questions, and how we try to answer them may say more about us than about the people we're judging.

No pitcher ever has it easy. *All* pitchers must work hard. *All* pitchers must refine their craft. It's almost never just about *stuff*. Dalkowski dreaming is no insult to the great pitchers who made it; from Pete Alexander to Max Scherzer, they have all earned their way up. And yet, if it is true that we can only do as much as we can do, then the journey would be more of an adventure, the ultimate triumph or defeat more noble, if like Dalkowski we lacked 100 percent of the confidence, the command, the self-possession, the commitment, the resistance to making bad decisions that so many great players possess—to be gloriously human. Or, to put it more succinctly, it would be fun to be able to throw as hard as any person ever has. Even if just for a moment, and even if nothing more came of it than that, no one could say you hadn't lived life to the fullest.

—Steven Goldman is an author of Baseball Prospectus.

A Reward For A Functioning Society

by Cory Frontin and Craig Goldstein

On July 5, Nationals reliever Sean Doolittle said in the middle of a press conference regarding the restart of Major League Baseball and what would later be known as summer camp, "sports are like the reward of a functioning society." This sentence was amidst a much longer, thoughtful reply about the societal and health conditions under which MLB players were being brought back. It's a very similar sentiment to one Jane McManus used on April 7, when she discussed the White House's meeting with sports commissioners. She said "sports are the effect of a functioning society—not the precursor."

Both versions of the same sentiment spoke to a laudable ideal in the context of a country that was not addressing a rampaging virus, and opting instead to bring sports back for the feeling of normalcy rather than the reality of it. "Priorities," as McManus said.

On Wednesday, the NBA's Milwaukee Bucks conducted a wildcat/political strike, refusing to come out for Game 5 of their playoff series against the Orlando Magic. The Magic refused to accept the forfeit, and shortly thereafter other playoff series were threatened by player strikes. Eventually the league moved to postpone that day's games, folding to players leveraging their united power.

The backdrop against which these actions took place was the shooting by police of Jacob Blake. Blake was shot in the back seven times by police, as he attempted to get into his vehicle. He managed to survive the assault, but is paralyzed from the waist down.

⚾ ⚾ ⚾

The step taken to walk out, first by the Milwaukee Bucks, then subsequently by other NBA, WNBA, and MLB teams, was a step toward upholding the virtue of the sentiment described by McManus and Doolittle. But that sentiment does not align with the broad history of sports in this and other countries, a history that contradicts the core of the idealistic statement.

Sports have been a significant part of American society for most of its existence, expanding in importance and influence in recent years. The idea that society was functioning in a way that was worthy of the reward of sports for most of that time is laughable. Much of America is not functioning and has not functioned for Black people, full stop. The oppressed people at the center of this political act by players, specifically Black players, in concert throughout the NBA and in fits and starts throughout Major League Baseball, have not known a society that functions for them rather than *because* of them.

Politics has been part of the sports landscape since the inception of sport, but for just about as long people have bemoaned its presence. Sports are to be an escape, it is said. An escape from what, though? A functioning society?

No, the presence of sports has never signified a cultural or political system that is on the up and up. Rather, the presence of sports *reflect and reinforce the society that produces them.*

⚾ ⚾ ⚾

The Negro Leagues were born out of societal dysfunction. The need for entirely separate leagues, composed of Black and Latino players barred from the Major Leagues because of racism? That is not a functioning society, and yet there were sports.

Even the integration of players from the Negro Leagues resulted in a transfer of power and wealth from Black-owned businesses and communities and into white ones, mirroring the dysfunction that had bled into every aspect of American society at the time. Japheth Knopp noted in the Spring 2016 Baseball Research Journal:

> *The manner in which integration in baseball—and in American businesses generally—occurred was not the only model which was possible. It was likely not even the best approach available, but rather served the needs of those in already privileged positions who were able to control not only the manner in which desegregation occurred, but the public perception of it as well in order to exploit the situation for financial gain. Indeed, the very word integration may not be the most applicable in this context because what actually transpired was not so much the fair and equitable combination of two subcultures into one equal and more homogenous group, but rather the reluctant allowance—under certain preconditions—for African Americans to be assimilated into white society.*

To understand the value of a movement, though, is not to understand how it is co-opted by ownership, but to know the people it brings together and what they demand. When Jackie Robinson—the player who demarcated the inevitability of the end of the Negro leagues—attended the March on Washington for Jobs and Freedom in 1963, he did so with his family and marched alongside the people. He stood alongside hundreds of thousands to fight for their common civil and labor rights. "The moral arc of the universe is long," many freedom fighters have echoed, "but it bends towards justice." The bend, it is less frequently said, happens when a great mass of people place the moral arc of the universe on their knee and apply force, as Jackie, his family, and thousands of others did that day.

⚾   ⚾   ⚾

Of course, taking the moral arc of the universe down from the mantle and bending it is not without risk. Perhaps the outsized influence of athletes is itself a mark of a dysfunctional society, but, nonetheless, hundreds of athletes woke up on Wednesday morning with the power to bring in millions of dollars in revenues. That very power, as we would come to find out, was matched with the equal and opposite power to *not* bring those revenues. That power, in hands ranging from the Milwaukee Bucks, to Kenny Smith in the *Inside the NBA* Studio, from the unexpected ally, Josh Hader, and his largely white teammates to the notably Black Seattle Mariners, would be exercised for a single demand: the end to state violence against Black people. Not unlike the March itself, it sat at the intersection of the civil rights of Black Americans and bold labor action. The March on Washington stood in the face of a false notion of integration—against an integration of extraction but not one of equality—and proposed something different. Just the same, the acts of solidarity of August 26, 2020 will be remembered in stark defiance of MLB's BLM-branded, but ultimately empty displays on opening weekend.

Bold defiance like this can never be without risk. By choosing to exercise this power, the Milwaukee Bucks took a risk. They risked vitriol and backlash from those they disagreed with. They risked fines or seeing their contracts voided, as a walkout like this is prohibited by their CBA. They risked forfeiting a playoff game, one that, as the No. 1 seed in the playoffs, they'd worked all year to attain. They didn't know how Orlando would respond. It wasn't clear that other teams throughout the league would follow suit in solidarity. And it wasn't known the league would accept these actions and moderately co-opt them by "postponing" games that would have featured no players.

If the league reschedules the games, some of the athletes' risk—their shared sacrifice—will be diminished, in retrospect. But they did not know any of that when they took that risk. And it is often left to athletes to take these risks when others in society won't, especially those of their same socioeconomic status and levels of influence.

It is athletes, specifically BIPOC athletes, that take them, though, because they live with the risk of being something other than white in this country every day. They are no strangers to the realities of police brutality. It seems incongruous then, to say that sports are a reward for a functioning society when we rely on athletes to lead us closer to being a functioning society. Luckily, our beloved athletes, WNBA players first and foremost among them, understand what sports truly are: a pipebender for the moral arc of the universe. ∎

—Craig Goldstein is editor in chief of Baseball Prospectus. Cory Frontin is an author of Baseball Prospectus.

Index of Names

Almonte, Yency 40
Bard, Daniel 42
Bernabel, Warming 92
Blackmon, Charlie 16
Bowden, Ben 77
Castellani, Ryan 44
Cron, C.J. 68
Daza, Yonathan 69
Decolati, Niko 69
Desmond, Ian 70
Díaz, Elias 18
Díaz, Jairo 46
Diehl, Phillip 78
Doyle, Brenton 89
Estévez, Carlos 48
Freeland, Kyle 50
Fuentes, Josh 20
Gilbreath, Lucas 92
Givens, Mychal 52
Gomber, Austin 54
González, Chi Chi 56
Gray, Jon 58
Hampson, Garrett 22
Hilliard, Sam 24
Kauffmann, Karl 91
Kemp, Matt 26
Kinley, Tyler 60
Lambert, Peter 78
Lavigne, Grant 70
Márquez, Germán 62
McMahon, Chris 88
McMahon, Ryan 28
Montero, Elehuris 71
Murphy, Daniel 30
Oberg, Scott 79
Owings, Chris 32
Pillar, Kevin 34
Pint, Riley 92
Ramos, AJ 79
Ramos, Roberto 72
Rodgers, Brendan 73
Rolison, Ryan 80, 86
Romo, Drew 74, 90
Santos, Antonio 81
Schunk, Aaron 74, 88
Senzatela, Antonio 64
Sosa, Henry 82
Stephenson, Robert 66
Story, Trevor 36
Tapia, Raimel 38
Tinoco, Jesus 82
Toglia, Michael 75, 87
Veen, Zac 75, 85
Vilade, Ryan 76, 86
Weatherly, Sam 91
Welker, Colton 76, 89

For the Joy of Keeping Score

THIRTY81 Project is an ongoing graphic design project focused on the ballparks of baseball. Since being established in 2013, scorecards have been a fundemental part of the effort. Each two-page card is uniquely ballpark-centric — there are 30 variants — and designed with both beginning and veteran scorekeepers in mind. Evolving over the years with suggestions from fans, broadcasters, and official scorers, the sheets are freely available to everyone as printable letter-size PDFs at the project webshop: www.THIRTY81Project.com

Download, Print, Score, Repeat ...

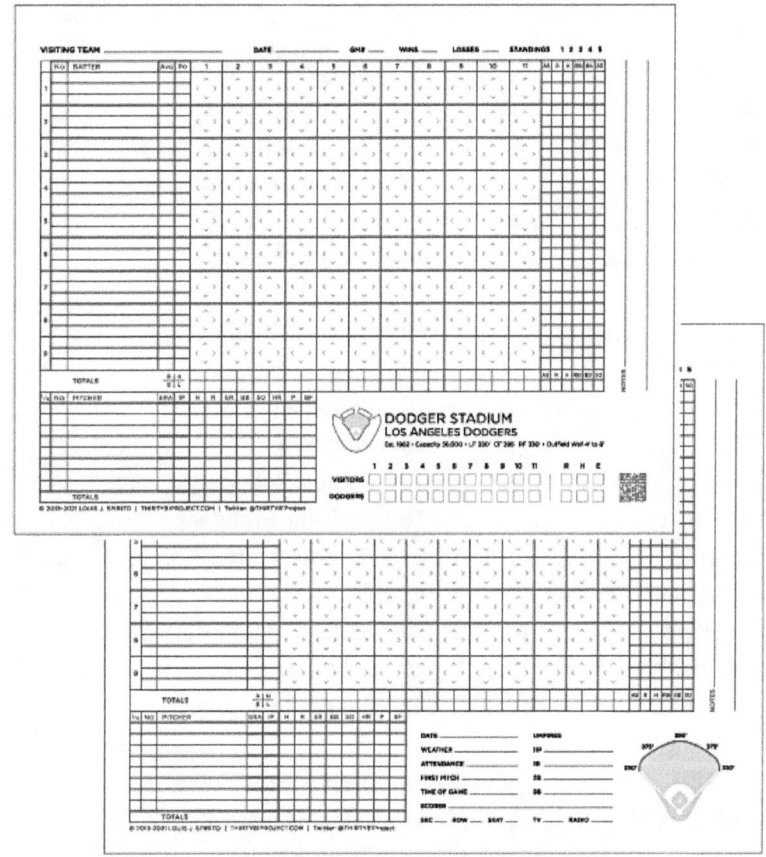

Scorecard design ©2013-2021 Louis J. Spirito | THIRTY81Project